*Alice Princess--*

*an Autobiography*

Hulme and Alice Siwundhla as
they graduated from college.

# Alice Princess --

## an Autobiography

*by* ALICE PRINCESS SIWUNDHLA

Pacific Press Publishing Association
Mountain View, California
Omaha, Nebraska

# Dedication

*To the sacred memory of the late*
*Lowell A. Edwards, the greatest and*
*kindest man I ever knew.*

*First printing, September, 1965—17,500*

*Second printing, February, 1966—10,000*

Library of Congress
Catalog Card No. 65-25620

# Preface

No one is lost to the sight of God. If you do not believe this statement, you have not heard the story of Alice Princess Siwundhla.

Alice knew the road to enlightenment lay always before her, though much of that road proved dark and treacherous. It was a road mired in tribal superstitions and heathen customs that only a girl with the will of Alice Princess could surmount. She little knew where or how far the road might lead, but that didn't keep her from searching.

First it led from the mud-floored hut of her orphaned childhood in Nyasaland, Africa, to the mission at Malamulo. Eventually it led to an airplane at Salisbury, Southern Rhodesia. Then, with the speed of a miracle, her way opened on new and exciting vistas: Nairobi, Khartoum, Rome, London, and Los Angeles.

That's where I first met Alice, on our television stage in Hollywood before a nationwide TV audience viewing "This Is Your Life." She was a radiantly alive young lady accompanied by her handsome, steadfast husband, Hulme, and their two adorable children. (They now have a third equally fine child.) I told Alice, as she sat in the well-known couch on our stage, that the great and the small of our land had been honored in that seat, but never one who had come so far in miles and mental and social adjustment as she. I was thinking, "And, I'll bet, never one better able to make the adjustment."

Needless to say, hers was one of the most inspiring lives of all the 425 we presented through the years. But, a mere half hour! We could have used five hours and still not told all the story of this young lady so endowed with courage and faith.

That is why I am delighted that Alice finally has put her own life into words. This book, as none before it, tells from a young girl's point of view of the stark primitiveness of life in a tiny African village; of the life she faced when her father's death left her an orphan; of how she and her sister fled to her grandmother's village. Alice's enthusiasm for life is contagious. You'll find it highly exciting to share her elation as she tells of meeting her brother and sister and earlier mission workers in surprise reunions on our stage.

Thirst for spiritual enlightenment has been a part of Alice's inner makeup since she stole away from the primitive tribal drums of her African village and followed the sound of the mission bells to the chapel in Luwazi. There she was discovered sitting coolly and serenely, a little orphan girl in a dress much too small for her. I am sure the engaging smile and Alice-in-Wonderland-like charm that bubbled forth for all of us that night on "This Is Your Life," when Alice Princess reacted to the wonders of being on a television stage in America, must not have been unlike the reaction that greeted the missionaries who found her at Luwazi.

The heroes and heroines of this true narrative, aside from the Siwundhlas, are the missionaries who do so much with so little recognition. What deeds of courage and compassion these selfless men and women perform to bring light to the forgotten areas of our world!

I saw Alice just the other day. She's still the effervescent but gracious girl we met nine years ago; the only difference is that which higher education brings to a mind hungering for learning. She's still a princess, but one who gets her three hearty children off to school, then her husband, then herself. She and Hulme are working hard, for they are still on the road to high achievement. And do you know where it leads? Right back to Africa, to the very beginning of the trail—the huts and flies and tribal drums. For this is Alice; she must go back to tell other young girls and boys: No one is lost to the sight of God.

The road will be easier to travel now, for Hulme will be with her; two young, dedicated people returning to their native land one day— soon, perhaps—as teachers.

Which will be greater: Africa's gain or America's loss?

RALPH EDWARDS.

Hollywood, California
May 20, 1965

# 1.

As a young man, Father, a Mtumbuka tribesman from the region of Lake Nyasa, left his brothers and sisters to live out their lives by the old patterns, while he traveled hundreds of miles to Johannesburg looking for something better. There, instead of laboring in the mines, he trained as an orderly and secured work in the huge City Deep Hospital.

At the hospital he met Mother, who had taken nurses' training there. They fell in love, married, and set up a home which, for Africans, was modern and comfortable. She had always used beds, chairs, blankets, and sheets, but he found such luxuries a source of wonderment and delight.

Father, whom we called Tata, made a handsome figure in his white orderly's uniform. His features were not heavy. He had a thin nose, thin lips, and deep-set eyes. His long, slender fingers resembled those of an artisan.

We called Mother Umame. She had a slim, pretty face with liquid brown eyes, and she spoke with a soft voice. Father could almost span her slim waist with his two hands spread out. "As tiny as the *namwali* [maiden]!" he would say, proud that his wife kept her girlish figure while other women grew fat as mealie mush.

In the sunny days of my early childhood I played with Tillie, my older sister, in the small yard of our red brick cottage, which belonged to the hospital. Afternoons we looked for the coming of Umame and Tata from their work in the hospital. Life for us was a sweet round of play, sliding down the great mine dumps of Johannesburg. Life meant sound sleep, warm baths, good soup, and fresh mealies and porridge.

When I reached the age of six, I walked with Tillie to the school operated by City Deep. A neighbor kept Camie, our baby brother, but Tillie and I took care of ourselves. When we returned from school, we had housework to do, and Tillie saw that I did my share.

One clammy day in June, Umame came home hoarse with a cold. It got worse rapidly. She took all kinds of remedies, wrapped up her throat, and bathed her feet; but still she coughed a lot every day. She did not stop work, for the hospital was overflowing with the sick. Then pneumonia struck her, and we had no miracle drugs in those days.

Tata had to take her to the hospital. He knew she could not live, and he nearly went wild with grief. He loved Umame devotedly; he had often brought her gifts and treats. Now he walked the floor weeping like a child.

Then one morning they brought my mother, my precious Umame, home in a box shaped like the sole of a shoe. We stood around and watched, too stunned to understand. They arranged the box on trestles in our sitting room. Tightly clutching Tillie's hand, I followed them in, puzzled and worried. I stood on my tip-toes trying to see what was in that box. Father lifted me up, and to my horror I saw our mother. She lay so very still with her smooth, pretty hands folded. I looked at those hands especially, for they had spanked me. Even though I had cried and jumped up and down, I knew those hands meant love for me, and provision, and sympathy.

Her black hair, parted in the middle, lay smoothed down by her small, pretty ears. As Father held me there, I looked and looked; but her eyes did not open, nor did her lips curve in their accustomed smile. It seemed that she should wake up at any moment and say something, but she didn't.

That same day they took my Umame out and buried her in a bleak place provided for mine workers outside the city. I screamed and cried. I clutched and tore at my little chest with one hand, while Tillie held the other tightly. June is cold and windy south of the equator. The wind cut like a knife on that dreadful day. I noticed one of the men's coats billowing in the piercing wind.

More piercing than the wind came the thought that my mother was gone, gone! A part of me died with her that day.

As the night came at the end of that awful day, Father tucked us into bed. But how we missed Mother! She had always kissed us good night. Even when she had to be on duty when we went to bed, she assured us that she would kiss us when she returned.

Until we lost her, such a frightful thing as not having a mother had never entered my imagination. I had taken our neatly made beds, polished floors, and ironed pinafores for granted. Already our little house suffered for her loss. Dust rolled itself into balls under the beds. In the kitchen stacks of dirty plates, smeared with dried gravy and mealie porridge, grew bigger. The tablecloth was eggy and rumpled. Clumsy, careless feet ground hunks of mud into her polished linoleum. I had never seen our home dirty before.

The happy days had gone. Mother would no longer stand by our table in the kitchen preparing hominy or beating up sweet-cakes. She would no longer wash and iron our little clothes or change our grimy sheets or send us to Sunday school. Never again would she put on her stiff white uniform with the flowing, filmy veil to go to work at the hospital. Mother had been a lovely nurse, and I had felt proud of her neat person. I wanted to be a nurse like Umame.

Camie, my baby brother, probably suffered more than I. He had never been left wet and dirty before. He had always enjoyed his bath and warm milk and cuddling, and he had slept in a clean little cot.

As the days passed, Tata had to send us here and there for someone to care for us. It is a wonder one or two of us did not die. When we ran home from school, Tillie would go to the place where Camie was staying and get him, and take him home with us—not the shiny home of our mother's day, but just home. Tillie, eager and anxious to make things bright, scrubbed as well as she could. Father would come home in his white jacket from the hospital and help Tillie prepare the meals. I fetched the water and dried the dishes.

Father brought home bread and little flat tins of sardines packed in oil. He would mash them down on slices of bread, let us drink hot coffee with milk and sugar in it. We would prepare *mnqusho* (hominy) on Monday, rice on Tuesday, potatoes on Wednesday, maize on Thursday, pumpkin on Friday. Then we started over again. We ate meat on Saturday, and with Father's help we managed a good Sunday dinner with pork, mutton, or some cheap cut of beef. Sometimes we had chicken.

# 2.

AT FIRST I didn't notice it, for little children do not always observe such things, but Father began to be sick. I remember hearing him cough hard in the night. My sister would get up and pour him a cup of coffee from the pot we always kept stewing on the back of the kitchen stove. Before the grass had grown four years on Mother's grave, Father had to quit his work at the hospital.

He began to pack for a long journey. We had no idea about where we were going, or when, or why. We plied him with eager questions. After a little exertion he would sit down, the sweat pouring from his face, and try so hard to answer us.

"We're going to my home up in the north, in the Vypsya country, where it is warmer than here," he answered us with a faraway look in his eyes. Strange, he had never told us much about it before. We could not understand his troubled look, but we jumped up and down with excitement at the thought of a trip.

"Is it nice? Do we have a grandmother?" we asked. My sister asked more questions, for she had a more orderly mind than I.

A strange look came into Father's kind eyes.

"You won't think it very nice," he told us. "I am afraid you won't like it at all. Yet I knew no other home until I came to Johannesburg. There are good things about it: the warm weather, the water nearby, and the clean, sandy beaches where I can rest and get well. The doctors say that rest and sunshine is the best cure for the sickness I have. I must get well to take care of you."

"But our grandmother—" Tillie objected. "I want a grandmother like Jeanie's and Hilda's. I want one who can make sweetcakes and pudding for us and who can sew new dresses for us. See? Our dresses are too small, the ones Mother made. I'm glad you're taking us to our grandmother."

A still queerer look came into his eyes. "Your grandmother never saw a sewing machine in her life, or a stove, or a pudding dish," he replied shortly. "But she is my mother and I love her. You will have to try to understand her and be kind to her. She is very different from your Umame."

Tillie and I talked about this queer thing. What a funny grandmother that must be—not to sew dresses or bake bread and sweetcakes!

After Father got men to help him ship off his belongings, some people allowed us to sleep in a vacant house in Sophiatown while we waited for a place on the train. Friends brought in mattresses for us, and we unrolled our blankets and lay down. Tillie and I whispered awhile about how strange we felt at leaving the only home we ever had known. Tillie, with her mouth close to my ear, whispered something that turned my heart to ice.

"It doesn't seem right, Sister, to leave Mother here all alone. Who'll put flowers on her grave? Who'll pull the long grass and clean off the place?"

I pondered that, though I longed to reach the clean white sand and the bright water Father talked about.

I do not know how long we had slept when shouts awakened us. Then, suddenly a bullet whizzed into the room and buried itself in the ceiling above our bed. Father jumped up, dumped us onto the floor, and covered us with the mattress.

"Stay there!" he ordered. "Don't get out till I tell you." The bullets poured into the room, some even penetrating the mattresses under which we trembled. We didn't dare cry.

At last things quieted down, and we must have slept. Father later told us that two men had been quarreling over a woman. Father said he was glad to be getting us out of Johannesburg.

Of course we had to travel in the native section of the train. People seemed to think that the color of our skin made us impervious to hardship and misery. We suffered tortures for water, for thirsty passengers had emptied the drinking cooler almost as soon as we boarded the train. The plain wood seats and the filthy floors added to our discomfort. The soot blew into our car, which was close to the engine. Once on the wretched journey I thought of the mashed sardines and the fat slices of bread Father used to butter and cover with peach jam. The vision so tantalized me that I cried for sardines and bread, but Father hushed me sharply.

"You know I couldn't buy a sardine now if I had a thousand pounds sterling. No more crying or I'll spank you. I'm doing all I can," he said, and shook me a little.

Camie, in rumpled, soiled rompers, lay asleep in Father's lap. Father, looking haggard and thin, coughed almost constantly.

The landscape, now wild and beautiful, now dreary and rocky, fled past the windows. Once I saw a herd of impala running gracefully and leaping across the bushveld. Several times we saw zebras and elephants.

At the shore town of Chipoka we took a lake steamer. To Father's relief the things shipped from Johannesburg had arrived, so we could take them on the boat with us. We had brought Mother's linens, dishes, pots, and kettles in boxes, along with her sewing machine, a gramophone, pictures, Big Ben chiming clock, and other treasures. Tillie and I suffered seasickness at first; we couldn't stand the roll and toss of the boat. But after a day we were better, and ran and played everywhere.

Father lay on the deck with little Camie playing quietly by his side. We reached our journey's end after three weeks of travel from Johannesburg.

# 3.

WHEN we got to Father's village, the people came out of the huts and surrounded us. Father stood there swaying, trying to stand up and talk with them in their own queer language. Tillie and I, heartsick, understood not a word the people said.

Father must have told them how tired he felt, for they took him to a hut and spread a mat for him. Tillie ran with a waterpot to the lake, brought water, and washed our thin, tired Tata's face and neck and arms. Then she took off his shoes and bathed his tired feet. She used a washrag and a towel from our suitcase.

He had hired carriers to bring our boxes from the steamer. The men piled them up in the back of the hut the people had assigned us. The huts, made of mud and thatched with grass, scared me. "We can't live here," I whispered to Tillie. "There are no beds or chairs or tables!"

"You be *still,*" Tillie commanded in the Xhosa language. "We can do anything to help Tata get well. When he gets well, we can go back. You're not to make him sick with crying around, either!" At last I began to understand that Father had come here to get well, not to stay. Tillie told me he had a coughing disease called tuberculosis which could be cured sometimes by rest, sunshine, and eating fruit.

Our Gogo (grandmother) horrified me. She wore her hair shaved close to her head, so she did not look quite like a woman. Her earlobes had been pierced, also her lips. She made no effort to cover her empty, flabby breasts, and seemed not to care. Her feet were horny and bare. Still, she treated us kindly, even if she did not look the way grandmothers should. She seemed glad to see Father, and talked long and loudly with him in that queer language we did not understand.

8

"She is my mother and I love her," Tata had said.

"Poor Tata!" I thought. "My Umame was so lovely, so beautiful. No wonder he never talked much of his mother or the Vypsya country when we lived in Johannesburg."

After a while we began to get used to the strange foods and customs of the village. Instead of fluffy bread from the City Deep bakery, with butter and jam, we had *nsima*—stiff, half-cooked cornmeal mush. The *nsima,* containing no salt, we ate with a salty *ndiwo* (relish). The *ndiwo* contained vegetables or meat or a mixture of both. Some people caught rats and mice to eat, but Father sternly told us never to eat food like that. He also frowned on eating fried ants.

Mostly we ate fish. This we roasted in coals after wrapping it with leaves and a layer of clay. The fish tasted good, but only slowly did we get used to the tasteless, starchy *nsima*. We would pick off a piece of it and dip it into the salty *ndiwo*. No spoons, plates, forks, or knives.

When I complained to Tillie, she retorted, "I remember a certain *namwali* who used to cry to get out of washing dishes."

I thought I would never complain again if only we could live as in the dear, happy days at City Deep.

The villagers held strange beliefs, too, that we didn't understand: Twin babies brought a curse and ought to die. The mother ought to die, too, if the government didn't interfere and make so much trouble. The arrival of twins proved that the mother had another lover besides her husband. We learned that for a girl in her menses, or a woman *ndi mimba* (expecting), to touch salt meant almost certain death. Whole families could die from a thing like that.

Taking pictures was an evil, too. Father's tribe had not seen much of photography, but they held it in great horror. If a man died in a house, it must be abandoned or torn down.

These people held beer dances—wild, sensual orgies which our father forbade us to attend.

We didn't like the primitive mud houses without beds, tables,

or chairs; but we learned to endure the lack. We spent most of
our time outside in the bright, warm sunlight. Father lay in the
sun a great deal, while Tillie took care of him. She would often
tell me to go and sit by him.

"He misses Umame," she would say to me, shaking her head
wisely. "I know if Umame were alive, he would get well very
soon. She always knew just what to do! Oh, she would make some
scones, and some pudding with jelly on top, and have some
roasted white potatoes. But I cannot cook so well, Alice, without
a Fredonia stove."

I nodded, for I, too, remembered Umame and the secure days
in our small brick house. In fact, I dreamed of them again and
again in the night. Then when I woke up, I would be lying on
a mat in a mud hut in the Vypsya country, while Father coughed
pitifully.

# 4.

FATHER felt well enough that fall to return to work in Johannesburg. He left us in Blantyre, where we attended school at the Church of Scotland Mission that year. There we smiled and laughed more. We found things cleaner and more orderly than in a heathen village. We saw grandmothers, too, who could knit and sew and read and write, and who did not chew tobacco or dip snuff. Tillie often told me to watch people like that. "We must remember to be like our Umame," she reminded me.

Blantyre Mission, we learned, was established in the year 1876 by Harvey Henderson. The Church of Scotland built the mission to educate and evangelize the Africans. The first trading store in the country still did business nearby.

David Livingstone, in his fierce battle against the slave traffic of the Portuguese and the Arabs, realized that trade was essential. The Arabs and Portuguese offered sorely needed tradestuffs only in exchange for "black ivory"—slaves. Livingstone argued that the way to cut down the tribal wars, often instigated to get slaves to trade, was to bring in legitimate trade.

Tillie and I often walked down to the first big store brought in by two Scotchmen, the Moir brothers. It was called *Mandala* because in the Cinyanja language, the wavering reflection one sees in water is *mandala*. One of the Moir brothers was nearsighted and wore glasses. Looking into the spectacles, the fearful natives saw their *mandala* and gave that name to the store, and to all of the African Lakes Stores.

The store had a wall around it like that of a fort. We were told that in the early days there was much fighting. We were disappointed in Mandala, though. It was nothing like the shops and *ticky* (threepence) bazaars we had seen in Johannesburg.

Tillie wrote letters in answer to Father's letters. He told us he was working, and sent money and cloth for dresses. The ladies at the school helped us to make them. We began to feel much happier.

Then for a long period we heard nothing more from dear Tata. Our anguish was terrible. Finally a letter came, scrawled with a trembling hand. He was not working, he wrote. Weeks later he wrote again, telling us he had gotten sick as before. The cold climate of Johannesburg, together with grief, worry, and hard toil, were exacting their price. This time Father was so ill he could hardly endure the journey northward.

One day without warning our father came staggering up the mission road. I had to look twice before I recognized him. Was this tottering skeleton our dear Ubaba? I could not help crying. His bony hands lingered on my head. *"Musalire, wokondedwa,"* he said, as if calling me "beloved" and telling me not to cry would help things.

"What is the matter? What is wrong, dear Ubaba?" I kept crying. Tillie ran quickly to the headmistress's cottage and came back with a cup of hot tea. When Tillie worried, she also did something about it. You could depend on her!

Tillie found a place for Father to rest, and the mission doctor examined him and gave him some medicine. "Better stay here, friend, and let us take care of you," the doctor advised.

When he left, he was shaking his head. Tillie and I saw him and went wild with anguish. With Umame gone we could not spare Tata!

"I'll save him! I'll save him!" Tillie screamed. "It's warmer up near the Vypsya. He must be warm. It is too cold here."

Even Tata, weak as he was, wanted to go. He felt that his only hope was in basking in the warm sand by the lake and resting and resting and resting. In spite of the kind offer of the missionaries, we packed our few things and left.

We took the boat again. This time Tillie and I sat by Tata all the way. Something told me that another change, even more terrible, was coming into our lives. And it did happen—not long after we got back to Nkata Bay, where our aunt Nyamukolongo lived. Tata began lying out in the sun as he had done before, but this time the slender flame had flickered too long to be revived. He had spent himself for us, and one night he died while we slept.

I know where the lonely heaped-up spot is, near Lake Nyasa, where dear Ubaba lies. A potsherd marks the spot where they lowered him, wrapped in a rough blanket and placed inside a hastily nailed-up box. When we heard the clods bumping there, it seemed that Tillie's heart and mine were torn out and buried there with him. We cried as we had never cried before, for Ubaba had been both mother and father to us since we lost our Umame. Now we had no one, and no prospect of anything but mud and ticks and flies and superstition and heathenism. Our tears streamed afresh as we gazed at the dirty village with its mud huts and clay pots and reed mats. How different from the happy life we had loved!

"Now we can never see Johannesburg again!" we mourned. "Never, never! We'll never have beds or tables or chairs or books or a stove like our Umame had! We'll not have hominy on Monday and meat and milk and cheese and bread and butter! Gogo never saw an apple or a peach or some grapes!"

Tillie later told me that Father died in terrible distress and worry about us. She said he prayed almost constantly that God would interpose to save us from the hopeless existence he knew faced us there. Once he had called us to him and told us he believed the great *Atate* (God) in heaven was going to answer his prayers.

"It will be after I am dead and am in my grave, my little ones," he told us in his faint voice. "But the great *Atate* will not leave you alone forever. He will remember you. Do not get impatient. Learn to wait on the Lord."

I still remember his dear face, marked with approaching death. Yet in his dark eyes I could read the message of his love and devotion. I will see my father again; of that I am sure.

# 5.

AFTER Father's grave was heaped high with sand, Tillie and I covered it over with pretty lake shells. All of our treasures were taken from us by relatives who felt they had a better right to Father's and Mother's things than we did. Because of superstition, the framed pictures of Mother and Father which had hung in our little parlor at home were burned, as were our other pictures we had in a box. They left us not a single likeness of Mother and Father to remind us of how they looked when they were alive and well and took care of us so tenderly. Though I would like to have saved some of those keepsakes, yet the sweet and holy memories I have of their lives are of far greater worth.

Without Tillie I wonder if I could have survived. I wonder now how little Camie, accustomed to sterilized bottles, snow-white diapers, and neat baby dresses *did* survive. Babies die easily in African villages, of a thousand things. Many a mother counts five, six, ten babes dead. Some lose count. The dangers lurking in filth and human and animal waste were unrecognized. Cruel poverty was everywhere. Of course nature was in a measure kind. We had warm weather much of the time. The clean sunlight spread like a healing blanket over rich and poor. The kindly lake lapping on the edge of the village gave us more cleanliness than we would have had in an inland village. We were in and out of the water all day long.

And Tillie was fierce with me if I struggled against the daily cleansing of my small body. She could slap me until it stung like bees and ants.

"Don't you forget Tata," she would scream, punctuating her words with slaps. "Don't you forget we lived in a pretty house, and we walked in shoes and went to church and read books!"

In spite of her vigilance, disease racked our bodies again and again. Tillie couldn't do everything, though her skinny form seemed to fly instead of walk much of the time.

In spite of all the obstacles, we were determined to rise above our surroundings. Something of Umame and Tata made us remain somewhat apart from the primitive ways of the village. And Tillie insisted that God *would* answer Tata's prayers. He *would* remember us.

A. TYSON-FLYN

Africans may wait for hours or even days for a train that rarely runs on schedule.

# 6.

THE houses in our village were of laced bamboo, overlaid with mud and thatched with grass. Very little light came in through the irregular window holes. When it rained for days on end, we shivered with cold and tried to cover ourselves with smelly straw mats and coarse pieces of cloth that smelled of cheap dye. We had pieces of bark cloth, too, rough and odorous. This was made by pounding the inner bark of the *mlombwa* tree. These covers were a far cry from Umame's fluffy blankets.

Tillie helped me remember what I might have forgotten: "We ought to be going to school, Sister. This life is no good. There is no light at the end. No one here knows how to live. Even the houses are wrong." She would shake her head decidedly.

"We had beds with sheets in our house at City Deep," she told me. "Umame used to make us little cakes sweet as honey, topped with sugar. Umame had a stove. Umame had long hair, put up with hairpins."

There was another Mandala store at the Bay, where they sold wondrous things. Sugar was there, brown and sweet from the sugar estates near Port Herald. Salt was sold, too. I used to stand and gaze greedily at the cups and plates and great rolls of cloth. I had lost hope of ever attaining anything, but I could look.

Tillie told me that our Umame had kept a tall brown jar full of sugar at Johannesburg. It was stored in a high cupboard beside the spices used for cakes and pies. We could not eat it as we wished, for Umame and Ubaba had said it would eat up our teeth and make us ill. Just the same, I'd have loved to put a big brown lump in my mouth once in a while and suck it slowly. Umame used to butter a big slice of bread and then sprinkle it with sugar. Oh, how good it was!

When we got up in the morning, we first rolled up our mats.
Then I tried to get away before my aunt or grandmother would
find me something to do. Not Tillie, though! She not only stayed
to help, but she ran with her skinny legs to get me. She'd always
find me, too, no matter where I hid. Then I had to help her hoe
or mud floors or gather sticks. Under Tillie's eye I could not go
far wrong; she was committed to keeping me straight.

Once I was convinced I ought to cut some decorations on my
stomach, as the other village girls did. "Your skin is smooth as a
snake," they told me. "You look horrible. You'll never catch a
husband. No man will want to marry a snake!"

They talked convincingly and showed me the remarkable decorations on their tummies. When their cuts were open and raw,
they rubbed charcoal into them; and when the wounds healed, the
ridgy scars remained.

"Doesn't it hurt?" I asked.

"Of course!" my friends said. "But it has to be. Our mothers
said so. Tillie just doesn't want you to be beautiful."

I yielded. When Tillie discovered what I'd done, she shouted at
me, beat me, and pinched me. I learned I'd better not do any more
things like that, for Tillie was fierce like a lioness when she got
angry.

Tillie loved beautiful things, though, bless her. She gathered
deep-purple crocuses and stuck them into the sand on Tata's grave.
She put some in her hair and mine, too, and told me of hats with
flowers on them that ladies wore in Johannesburg.

"They were wide and bright and beautiful," she said. "There
was a silk on them called 'ribbon' of bright colors. Our mother
wore a hat when she went to the *chalichi* with Ubaba and with
us. She looked very beautiful."

"What is '*chalichi*'?" I inquired. I knew what she would say,
for she had told me of her lovely memories of Umame and Ubaba
a thousand times. I never got tired of hearing them.

"*Chalichi*—" she whispered, "the English people always said
'church.' We dressed up in shiny black shoes and clean dresses. I

had a pink dress for church and blue and green dresses for school.
We walked carefully so we wouldn't get our shoes muddy or full
of dust. The church had long seats to sit in and kneel by when we
prayed. We went to the children's class, and we learned stories of
Jesus and of being good, and about David and the beanstalk, and
how Jesus gave some sardines to the multitude. Oh, Alice, it was
wonderful!"

At times Tillie would suddenly go silent and just think. Eventually I learned what she was doing—she was thinking about our
dear mother, so lovely, so neat, so kind; and she was busy evolving
plans for me and her and little Camie.

"She spanked me," Tillie once told me suddenly, interrupting
her reverie. Tillie hadn't said so, but I knew "she" meant our
Umame. "She had made a little pan of sweetcakes," Tillie continued, "and set them on our kitchen table for the frosting to
harden. We were going to have them when we came home from
*chalichi*. She left them there covered with a clean white cloth.

"I had on my best pink dress and so did you. I took one cake,
broke it in half, and gave some to you. We got frosting all around
our mouths and on our Sunday dresses. We had to wear our
school dresses to church, and I got a spanking besides." Tillie was
smiling. She loved to remember that spanking.

"Umame loved us truly," she told me. "When a umame loves,
she wants her children to grow up good and obedient. She had to
spank." She cocked her eye at me, and I knew what she was
thinking: She'd spank me, too, if I didn't walk the line.

Lots of the children in our village "ate" tobacco. That is, they
chewed it. Tillie lashed out against it, for Ubaba had warned her
against it before he died. "It spoils your lungs and teeth and tubes
and stomach," he told her. "It eats up money, and stinks. Never
use it, or let Sister or Brother use it. *Never!* Do you hear, Tillie?"

"I promise you, Tata," Tillie had said, her small mouth set in
a thin line. "I will beat Alice and Camie if they start that." She
meant it. The safest thing all around was to listen to Tillie.

When I showed signs of weakening on some heathen custom,

Tillie could be scathing. "Ha! you!" she'd greet me. "You with rat's teeth, a monkey's eyebrows, and duck's feet. Ha! You want an ox's mouth, too, chewing cud? Ha! I wish Umame were here to beat you. I will pull your hair till you won't have any left on your head." Once she did pull it, too, so hard that I remembered the pain for a long time. But Tillie was usually right, and I loved her with all my heart.

# 7.

TILLIE'S bright, beady eyes were on the lookout day and night for any way of bettering our condition—for any indication that our Ubaba's prayers were to come true. I might become weary of following a star, but never Tillie. I might doubt that some vague Personage beyond the clouds would intervene to improve our unhappy lot, but never she.

When our Gogo commanded Aunt Nyamukalongo to return us to Gogo's village, we were glad the old lady was able to force our aunt to take us. Strong-willed as Aunt Nyamukalongo was, Gogo was stronger. Our walk took several hours. The scenery was nothing special. We were used to seeing baboons and monkeys swinging in the scraggly bush trees. The dense underbrush along the way, we did not care to investigate. A leopard might be taking his nap there, or a viper slithering through it. Even the grass was dangerous. My sister pointed to ticks that stayed there, whose bite could cause the deadly typhus. We reached Gogo's village at last, tired and glad to rest and eat.

Near Blair Village, where our Gogo then lived, was the Luwazi Mission; and the day we arrived we heard the mission's bells ringing. At the sound, Tillie rushed excitedly in from the bush where she had been gathering wood. I was busy mudding the *khonde,* a job she had put me to. I sensed that something was significant about those bells, though I could not imagine what.

"Now, you, you *mlesi* [lazy one], you mud this *khonde* smooth while I'm gone or I'll pull your hair," she had commanded in her usual bossy way. I got angry, as I was mudding as fast as I could so I could get off to my play again. I had spotted a ripe papaya, too, off in the bush; a volunteer tree had sprung up where someone had spit seeds a year or two before. I wanted to get my teeth into that fruit before someone else found it. Oh, how good papayas were! The thick meat tasted like honey and mango, and was so cool and lovely.

Now Tillie came running into the *khonde*. "Sister!" she shouted, grabbing me. "Listen! Listen! There are bells again! We're near to a church, a *chalichi*. This day must be Sunday! It must be! I lose track of days here, but now I know it is a church day!" She was jumping up and down in her eagerness.

We learned later it was Saturday, and the people at the mission were what we called the *Akristu* of the Seventh Day. But that made no difference to my sister. It was a church. It was a step nearer to the God who would remember.

After a sharp dispute with our grandmother, Tillie washed herself, put on the best piece of cloth she could find, and was off to church. No one, Gogo included, could out-argue Tillie, because her memories of Tata and Umame strengthened her. People were superstitious about the dead, and Tillie took advantage of the fact. "Our Tata desires this," she would say quietly, and a finger of fear would touch the heart of her opponent. She had only to repeat wishes she was sure our parents must have had, and she usually got her way.

When anyone attempted to prevent her from going to church, Tillie knew how to throw a fit! She would jump up and down, cry, and screech, "These things are as our Tata wanted!" or, "Our Umame took us to church every week! She would like it so! She does not want us to grow up without the great *Atate!* We have to go, or our Umame and Ubaba will come back and trouble us—and trouble you, too!"

Of no avail were Gogo's arguments that the church was a kind of trap, like a snare used to catch rats and mice. She told Tillie and me that once they got you into the church, ha! then that was not enough. Then you went to *skulu*, where they coaxed girls and boys to learn foolishness. The old ways were the best ways. Who needed to read? Who needed to write? Who ever in the olden days sewed with *singano* and *thonje* (needle and thread)?

"Our Umame and our Tata both sent us to the *skulu* in Johannesburg. It is their will!" I shouted, catching the fever from Tillie. Gogo finally consented, and off we went to the girls' compound, called the *mpanda,* at Luwazi Mission. Tillie purred like a baby cheetah.

There we heard the familiar songs we used to sing in our home, though we sang them in a different language. The Lord's Prayer was repeated, which I had learned in Xhosa when only a child, but I had not said it for so long I could not remember it. When church was dismissed, a missionary lady, Mrs. Davy, invited Tillie and me to come again the following Sabbath. She also asked us if we could not come to the school.

After Father died, we had stopped going to school. We told this lady we were afraid to attend, for many people did not believe in girls going to school. No man wanted to marry a girl who was educated. They believed that educated girls talk back to their husbands, that they are lazy, proud, and disobedient.

The following Sabbath, after a little persuasion, Grandmother agreed for us to go to church again. But she reiterated that she would not have us going to their *skulu* to be ruined for good!

Later when the question of school came up again, our Gogo flatly refused for us to go. She waved her fists, shook her head, jumped up and down, and shouted. I looked at Tillie. She had that stubborn, unbeatable look on her face, and my heart gave a little leap. Tillie would have browbeaten a lion or a leopard. I knew right then she'd win out and that we'd go to school.

And we did! After some maneuvers by Tillie, some talks by the mission director with our chief, and a few placating presents to Gogo, we found ourselves at Luwazi Mission Station. Oh, precious joy! In a wise, knowing atmosphere again, that same air that had surrounded our Ubaba. He was wise, inquiring, and knowing. He read books and despised superstition and ignorance.

That first evening was wonderful. We got water, made supper, and attended devotions with the other girls. Tillie got us some blankets with a little of Ubaba's money she had hidden. As Tillie and I were lying there on our mats, she put her arms around me and whispered, "See, Sister? I told you God would not forget. Our Ubaba said He would not, and I knew He would remember if we would be patient and wait for Him."

How I loved Tillie! She was so wise and so good. I could not have lived without her.

# 8.

MY HOME for several years was a room in the girls' home compound with a number of other students. At most mission stations, at least in parts of Africa where I have been, these compounds, or dormitories, are composed of a number of native houses. These are built the same as in the village, except that our window holes were larger and we had the luxury of window glass. Thus we had more light and more protection from cold and rain. Inside we had homemade chairs and tables made of native pit-sawn lumber. The floor was of mud, replaced often so it was kept smooth. We took turns mudding the floors.

Throughout our compound were fruit trees from which we could pluck and eat as we needed. Our missionary gave us each a garden plot, too, so we could grow vegetables to add to our *nsima* and bean *ndiwo*. I delighted in my garden of *cimanga* (maize), peas, sweet potatoes, eggplant, peppers, onions, and okra. Tillie's garden was even more imposing. She was so determined that I used to think she could grow a leopard if she happened to want one.

Our brother, Cameron, was down by Lake Nyasa with Father's cousins and brothers, where he had been taken long before. He learned to like swimming and fishing, and was settling down to the easy, indolent life of a *Msisya* native. But Tillie was determined to rescue him and bring him to school, and her steamroller will started up again. So we got permission and went up to Usiya in a canoe on lovely Lake Nyasa. We found Camie and told him of our excitement at attending school and church. We tried to show him this was the wonderful answer to our prayers, and the fulfillment of Tata's hopes.

But Camie showed no interest. He had been a nursing baby

when Umame died, and he had no recollection of her. He could hardly remember Ubaba either, and cared nothing for the impassioned promises Ubaba had exacted from Tillie.

"This is the life, Sister," Camie would whisper to me. "Don't listen to Tillie. She is foolish. The life she wants is hard and has few rewards. How do you know about this God? Who has ever seen Him?"

He had a strange influence over me. He took me fishing, and we would cook the fish over little fires and eat it in happy comradeship. Tillie and I stayed with our brother for four weeks. When it was time to return for the second semester I had become so enamored with the easy life that I refused to go back.

My poor sister returned to school alone. I don't know why she gave up so quickly; probably she was tired of trying to provide the backbone for the three of us.

I soon tired of the easy life. Six months later I decided to leave Camie and return to Luwazi Mission. When I met Tillie, she screamed with joy and pranced up and down the compound singing and shouting.

I was a little older by then, and I began to see things Tillie's way. I had been up at Usisya long enough to see that life there held no promise for anyone who had ambition, and I had it in me to be different. So I began to burn with ambition, just as Tillie had, to rescue my brother. My backbone began to stiffen.

Camie was more than a prisoner, for he did not even know he was bad off. He didn't want to be rescued. We had to sell him the idea first. I wondered if pinching and pulling hair, or even a slapping, might help.

I had to make another trip to see Camie. I was my sister's ally now. I went fierce as a lion, but gentle as a guinea fowl. Once more I tried to persuade our dear brother to come to school. I told him some wonderful stories from the Bible. At last Camie consented to come along. With other relatives whom I persuaded to seek a better life, our brother began school.

Mrs. Davy helped us all. I shall never forget how kind and

loving she was. Luwazi Mission was a beautiful place, and I began to appreciate school more and more. I sensed at last what Tillie had felt all the time—that there was a certain work ahead that God wanted us to do. Someway our father's prayers had done something special for us.

# 9.

*I* WORRIED a little about what Gogo and Aunt Nyamukalongo might do since we had decided to get all the schooling we could. But not Tillie! She worried not a bit. That girl held her small head high and flew at life like a mother hen protecting her chicks. If she got it into her head we ought to do a certain thing, Camie and I learned to do it. We always came to it in the end anyway. I never saw anyone with so much grit as Tillie.

Many customs among my people, though heathen, were honorable. One was insistence on the purity of the young girls. Some tribes, it is true, had low morals, even as do people in the slums of any country. But not so among the better class. Then, too, they honored the opinions of the old people. Young people did not presume to belittle or talk impertinently.

However, other customs were far from honorable, and Father knew them so well he had spent many days warning Tillie. She was too young to realize all that he was talking about, but she treasured his words, which she later came to understand. "Do not marry young," he counseled her. "Do not marry a man who has other wives. Marry a Christian. You will be sad if you do not. Do not let them force you or Sister into a marriage just because they offer many cattle."

Several times before I went to Malamulo, my people actually accepted part of the bride-price, or *lobola,* for my marriage. They were surprised and outraged at my refusals, for girls of the olden days were tame and obedient, and obeyed commands without question. The choice of a husband was for others to decide. This had been the custom for so long that girls up in the Vypsya country were aghast at our insolence.

But Tillie and I had had different advice. I had seen a better

life, and Tillie was with me. Our people naturally blamed education for my refusal to cooperate. Education, they said, makes girls
defiant and disobedient. They despaired of Tillie's and my getting husbands at all, and to them that was the supreme goal of a
woman.

One happy, holy experience came to Tillie and me before we
had been at Luwazi very long. It was one of the important steps
in our young lives. We both entered the hearer's class in the
church. This was organized for those who want to learn the doc-
trines of Christianity and who wish to study for two years before
baptism. There were so many things to learn and unlearn in Africa.

Christianity, good food, clothing, and security were changing
me. I was growing up. The life of our home village, the superstitions, the customs, led to nothing good, or grand, or great. In the
end, old people died in misery after a lifetime of it, leaving their
children no better off than they had been. The running, playing,
eating fish, hoeing, sleeping, dancing, were ends in themselves, and
led to nothing better. I began to see the uselessness of such a life.

Through our kind teachers, Bible study, and classes I had a
glimpse of a better way of life. There were Christian families on
the mission whose lives were far lovelier than those in the villages.
Men teachers, each with *one* wife, lived in neater houses. Their
voices were not loud and harsh. Their children were actually
prettier, or so it seemed to me. Their clothes were more attractive.
At night there were so many things to talk about—far more than in
an ordinary village. Missionaries brought in new, strange, and better ways of life. Books opened doors into thoughts, places, and
ideas that we had not previously known existed.

We learned ways to earn bits of money, too. Money bought
bright cloth from foreign lands, covered with flowers or vines or
stripes or dots of many colors. Money bought sugar and soap, and
how wondrous was soap! Long, long bars, as long as your arm,
from which you cut small segments to wash out your few pieces of
clothing. Money bought dishes. I'd seen some cups and saucers
at Mandala, which were so lovely I dreamed of them at night.

How I would love a cup and saucer all my own! Little girls even in Africa have their dreams.

When I told Tillie I dreamed of a cup and saucer, Tillie tossed her head. "Our Umame—" she began.

But I interrupted her. "If our Umame had so many things, why don't we have them now?"

It was then I learned that all our things had been taken from us. We had been only little girls. What did we matter?

"Where are they?" I cried. "What became of them? Where are the lovely things you are always telling me our Umame had?"

"They're all gone—all," she answered. "Only a pillowcase—they did not get that. I hid it. Long ago the dishes were broken. Some of the cups were covered with flowers—they were lovely. Umame stirred milk and sugar into coffee and tea and let us drink it out of pretty cups."

After Tillie and I were baptized, Tillie used our vacations preaching in the villages. She had no fear. She would go from village to village proclaiming Christianity to any audience that would hear her. And hear her they did; she saw to that.

Tillie had a certain little grace about her that always reminded me of Tata. Camie, too, looked like his Tata. As for me, they tell me I am the living image of Lena, my precious mother. I do not know; I can remember only the dim outline of her face. Yet her voice remains with me and always will, its loving cadences warming me, assuring me and lifting me up.

When I graduated from Luwazi, Pastor and Mrs. Davy told me I must go to the Malamulo Mission, almost 400 miles to the south. I had never seen it; though when Tillie and I attended the Church of Scotland Mission School, we had been only forty miles from it.

We had heard whispers about the famous Malamulo Hospital, too. We heard that a queer kind of magic in the hands of the Malamulo doctors and nurses could heal lepers, and that was something to think about. Lepers with no noses or ears or fingers or toes were no novelty. Until recently no one had dreamed there was a cure to this fearful disease. But there was at Malamulo. If you weren't too bad off you could be saved after two or three or four years of strong medicine. Tillie and I often talked about it. It was like reading about a miracle from the Bible.

Some of our relatives were strongly opposed to our getting any more education. They were loud and angry about it. They pointed out that this fancy education was blighting our lives. Then, too, they wanted to know, how long must they wait to eat our *lobola?* They willingly accepted all offers of marriage for me that promised a goodly number of cattle, for cattle were the wealth of central Africa. After going to the trouble of rearing a dead brother's girls, why shouldn't they profit by it? It was as simple as that. My comfort or my happiness, they reasoned, was none of my business.

Because of their insistence, men of all ages and stations showed up at the mission and called for me. They were the "middlemen" or marriage counselors, pleading the cases of young men, older men, and middle-aged ones, some of whom I knew had several other wives. Any one of them might have become my husband had it not been for the wondrous influence of Ubaba that reached out even beyond the grave to protect us.

I got tired of their pestering, for hardly a day went by that I was not approached by a messenger from my relatives. They were as determined to get control of my life as I was that they should not. If there had been no Luwazi Mission, what would have happened to me?

To my relatives' despair, I refused the men one and all. It was a relief for me to get out on the road with my small pack, headed for Malamulo, and away from unwelcome suitors, urging relatives, and angry villagers, all anxious to eat my *lobola.*

I had to walk seventeen miles to the dock, but what did it matter? We always were in danger even in the girls' compound where we slept at night. I had lived with danger all my life. The mosquito was as great a killer as the lion. Many a person succumbed to the tiny tick. Snakes got inside our houses in the compound. I have awakened many a time with rats chewing my heels.

Several of my friends from Luwazi Mission made the trip with me. We well knew there were crocodiles near the lake where we had to sleep en route to the Bay. There were lions and leopards all through the bush. At Nkata Bay, almost 400 miles from the famous school I had heard about, we stopped to wait for the *Mpasa,* the steamer which went to the southern harbor town of Chipoka. There we would await a ride on a slow-moving train that carried both freight and passengers to Blantyre, forty miles from Malamulo.

We tarried at night in rest houses. We had our blankets and mats, and could lie on the dirt floor to sleep. We were near to water for drinking and for cleansing ourselves. I had carried a small cookpot wrapped in my blanket, in which to prepare my food. In one place I slept on the clean sand, because the long wattle-and-daub house provided for sleeping was crawling with bed bugs, lice, and ticks left there by former travelers. Big cockroaches all but got on our food while we ate it, so hungry were they, and a rustling in the tall grass outside notified us that hungry rats were waiting, too. There were insects—biting, stinging, and sucking—a million of them, I am sure.

We faced life as it was because there was nothing else to do. I did not think too much of the hardships because our long, hard trip south was to better ourselves. It was going to be worth what it cost. We were climbing painfully and slowly up a steep ladder —so slippery and steep that many fell in the climbing. I hoped I had enough of my mother and father in me to reach the top, but I did not dream it would be so hard a climb.

I had seen many girls barely able to spell out words, hardly knowing how to hold a needle and thread, give up all their dreams and ambitions and marry. Soon they had babies on their backs, wrapped in dirty *nsarus.* They were dirty, drab, and loud-mouthed, and their schooling had gone for nothing.

My life was all that I had as my own. Yet so many were trying to order it for me, to take it out of my hands. People wanted me to marry so they could "eat my *lobola.*" That was a great price to pay, I thought bitterly, for a few slices of bloody, half-cooked meat, and a few lumbering, humpbacked cattle. My *life* for that? I would not give it!

We arrived in Blantyre on a Tuesday, the day when the missionaries went to town with Malamulo butter and other commodities. We had planned to walk the last forty miles, but we were glad to ride instead. Eagerly we got on the Malamulo lorry to ride out to the mission. We could almost see the end of our journey. We were so tired.

We passed through Limbe town with its train station. To our delight a luxury train passed through while we were there. I had ridden on a train long ago, second class, but had almost forgotten about it. We saw stores, too, and how we stared! Limbe was bigger than Nkata Bay, Mandala, or Kirkaldy, and it looked buzzing and wonderful to our countrified eyes.

We talked excitedly about what we would do if we had a little money. "I'd buy bread," cried one girl. "It is wondrous good, and the Europeans eat it with every bite they put in their mouths. And they have a *mafuta* to put on it called butter."

"Me, I'd get sugar," said another. "I'd get tea, too, and a good cup for my very own."

I said nothing, though my stomach was gnawing with hunger. I knew if I had money I would not buy bread or sugar. I would buy cloth, hungry though I was. I would buy cloth to put on my body instead of the faded, thin, sleazy stuff that was all I owned. Oh, how I would like the feel of lovely cloth all covered with flowers, stripes, or dots in lovely colors. I would have loved to have pretty, pretty, pretty dresses.

The lorry roared on as we talked. We had to hold on tight to the bags of meal or we'd have been thrown off. It seemed like a thousand years, we were longing to get there so much. Through Timketown we went over the river to Cholo, and then at last we passed by the Malamulo gate. The students call the gate "Come Again" because that is what was written on it. Somewhere down that red road was my Tillie and *skulu* and a promise of dreams come true. I think I would have started out running if my feet could have taken me any faster than the lorry, but my poor stomach ached with emptiness after three full days without food.

Wearily we trudged the last mile from the principal's house to the *mpanda*. The first building we saw was a brick mission house on the right. Someone told us it was Dona and Bwana Robinson's house. Then to the right was a square building with a *khonde* (porch) all around it. "The European Hospital," we were told. Our eyes took in everything. Next door to the hospital was a house of many chimneys and covered with cream-colored plaster—the house of the Bwana Doctor; and across the street lay the home of Bwana Principal. It looked like a palace. Lovely wicker chairs were on the porch and big ferns adorned the edge. Many kinds of flowers brightened the yard. Some boys with pieces of strap iron were cutting the grass. There was a great round thing by the kitchen door which I later learned was a 13,000-gallon water tank.

The road turned a little to the right. Below us lay the Indian hospital on the right and the African hospital and surgery on the left. People were coming and going continually. I saw American and English nurses dressed in gleaming white uniforms going between the surgery and the ward buildings. My heart always saddened when I saw a nurse, as I saw visions of Umame's loving face.

I drew a sudden breath and my heart filled with a sense of relief. At least here people were doing something about this thing called life. People here were living their lives in a better way. They had turned their backs on superstitions. The old ways were *not* good, at least *most* of them were not.

Past the huge Malamulo church and school and a couple of mission houses, we came to the gates of the *mpanda* where I knew Tillie must be. Suddenly I heard a terrific uproar, and weary as I was I sat down on the nearest stone and began to laugh. Tillie had seen me, and in her own way she was coming to greet me. It would take a color film with a sound track to capture Tillie as she really was. She swayed back and forth—half dancing, singing, improvising her own song of delight and welcome. Tillie, God bless her, could never do anything halfway. Like a queen she came—advancing by degrees, singing, retreating, dancing ahead, clapping her hands.

"*Mwana wa amama, mwana wa amama, eh eh eh wabwera!*"

"My mother's child, my mother's child, ha! ha! ha! she has come."

She conducted me as if I were visiting royalty to her *mpanda* hut, where she washed my sore feet and rubbed them with oil. She washed my face and hands, too. Thus she showed her loving concern and her joy at my arrival. She set food before me—food she had prepared in anticipation of this reunion. Snow-white *nsima* as only she could cook it, heaped high on a plate; delightful *ndiwo* of tomatoes, string beans, onions, and green peppers in a small earthen pot. For a special treat she served cooked bananas, ripe mangoes, and papayas, juicy and delicious. What a treat the papayas were for my starved stomach, and Tillie had chosen the best ones.

A. TYSON-FLYN

Boys attending Malamulo march to chapel service.

# 10.

AT MALAMULO I took the two-year domestic course. I learned how to knit, sew, and cook, and took courses in child care and housekeeping from Miss Ruth Foote. I was happier now than I had ever been, for I was learning to make pretty dresses and underclothes. I worked during vacation time to earn my school fees for the coming school year. I took in mending, did baby-sitting, and knitted for different people, even though I was poorly paid. I needed soap and other necessities.

Though I was happier than before, I still felt that something was lacking in my life. I had an empty feeling in my heart, especially when I saw some of my schoolmates with their parents. I wept many a night after I had rolled up in my blanket. I got lonelier each day, especially when dear Tillie was called away to Luwazi to teach school.

Missionaries came and went. We learned that some left Africa for the education of their children, or because they were old or sick, or perhaps they were sent to other mission fields. We often wished the missionaries would tell us more about how life was tackled on the other side of the world. We wished we could find someone who had an experience parallel with ours.

Now different missionaries had gone home and no new ones had come to Malamulo or Luwazi for several years. The very waters of the oceans about our huge continent were sown with mines, they told us, so that travel was hazardous and unsafe. A terrible world war raged, and dim echoes of its horrors reached even into the bush country of Central Africa. Then we learned that the atom bomb had blown Hiroshima and Nagasaki as high as the sky, and the war was over, at least for a while.

Every missionary who stood in classroom or pulpit told us that

Europe would never be the same again. We didn't understand
much about it, but it must have been important. We knew little
or nothing about Europe. It was hard to believe that war-wracked
segment of the world even existed. How could the boiling, seeth-
ing hatred that drenched the world ever touch us?

What more terrible thing could ever happen to Tillie and me
and Camie than had already happened? We were poor, insecure,
and wretched. Hearts get calloused to sorrow, it seemed. Though
I was going to school and dreaming of better things ahead, yet I
felt again and again that hopeless feeling tugging at my heart.
Somehow God had overlooked Tillie, Camie, and me, and in all
the rush of heaven and earth and sea and sky business, we three
little people had been forgotten. Why not? How could God, with
a war raging and a universe to attend to, remember three small
lives in the heart of dark Africa? And how could He attend to us
and to Esther Matuselah and to Sarapiah and all the others? How
could He answer prayers in Asia, Europe, America, Johannesburg,
Luwazi, and Malamulo? Despair settled down in my heart. I
couldn't see how God could care very much.

I ran everywhere in my spare time to earn a little money. I had
to have money for school fees and for cloth to cover my body.
Other girls had folks—poor, of course, but they managed school
fees and a Sabbath *nsaru,* or dress, and an everyday one as well.
There were some who had plenty.

I helped knit for Mrs. Higgins, dean of girls, and did mending
for Mrs. Ansley, the missionary nurse. I knitted for Miss Margaret
Johnson, the leper-colony nurse, and I sewed for others. Oh, dear,
the money came in agonizingly slow, and cloth at the Indian stores
at Mwalampanda was so high. It took days of knitting and sewing
to earn even one yard.

The cloth had come over from England and from India in great
boats, traveling thousands and thousands of miles, we were told.
Distance was hard to realize, but the 400 miles to Luwazi was very
real indeed.

They had a pretty yellow English cloth at Mwalampanda. Oh,

it was lovely! I worked and worked and saved and saved so I could have a Sabbath dress someday. I needed four yards of it and *thonje* (thread) and some buttons. Miss Foote had a pattern that I loved. It fitted at the waist and flared out to a full skirt. There was a new thing invented that we understood was a "zeeper." I still don't know how it works, but it does.

About that time Miss Foote went to America for a furlough. A lovely lady named Mrs. Agnes Vixie, the wife of Pastor Levi A. Vixie, came to take her place at the *mpanda*. She was very kind and gave me work to do so I could get some cloth for petticoats and other things I needed. Fresh courage crept into my heart. She didn't know the Cinyanja tongue, so she chose me as her assistant and interpreter. I was happier than I had been for a long time.

One day Mr. Higgins, our mission director, told us that another missionary couple was coming to Malamulo. Back of the boys' buildings a whole new village had been built of brick, made by our lepers. It was to accommodate new classes for young men who wanted to enter the gospel ministry. The new missionaries, even now on the way to Africa from America, were to direct the course. We were tremendously interested, for it was always interesting to see new missionaries come. (This is the reason ministers in Central Africa who went to hold revival meetings attracted such large crowds. The people were very, very curious! In many areas there were so few places to go, and so little excitement, that the people would go to see or hear anything unusual. It was a golden era for the spread of Christianity.)

We talked excitedly about the new missionaries to come. Would they be old, young, or middle-aged? Would they be so retiring that we would see little of them, or would they be enthusiastic and eagerly take us to their hearts?

Naturally we wished for this last kind; we had seen all kinds. It seemed so comfortable to have leaders who sort of breathed out a warmth that made the whole place seem hopeful and elevated. It was as if the door of heaven opened a bit.

Mr. Higgins kept telling us that the missionaries under appointment would soon be there. Then he would get word they were delayed. Then again they were coming. We wondered if they would ever arrive. Mr. Higgins told us that shipping companies and boats canceled bookings when they heard of any danger of mines the mine sweepers had missed.

We wondered much about this. Then we learned that a missionary *woman* was to have charge of the normal course. The young men who were to take the course murmured a lot about this, for it was well known that a woman's brain was not nearly as sharp or as clever as a man's brain. An *akazi* (woman) could never prepare her students properly for government examinations.

School opened. The teachers, except for the new missionaries, were there to start their classes. The evangelists' families had moved into the eight new houses. They had planted gardens, put up pigeon houses, and secured their allotments of notebooks and pencils. Still the new teachers did not arrive.

November passed. Christmas came. No one in the compounds knew how the outside world celebrated Christmas. We knew, but our dolls and toys were only dear memories. They had all been taken from us after Father died.

New Year's Day was a big holiday. We had games, races, marches, and a program on the *bwalo* (courtyard) in front of the school buildings.

New Year's Day, 1946, I put on my best dress, even though it was old and too small for me. I had patched it carefully under both arms. I scrubbed my feet and legs and tied a clean *mpango* over my head. We girls had a complicated march, filing in and out, crisscrossing, and stooping with water pots balanced on our heads. It was a great day, with a good feast at noon. It was fun.

We all went to school as usual on Wednesday. The evangelists and the normal students were asked, from the opening of school early in November, to visit standard six classes and learn all they could learn until the new teachers came. I heard them complaining that already two months had come and gone and nothing was started yet. Some grumbled that the new teachers were not coming at all, so the students were wasting their time.

On Thursday one of the boys of the teacher-training class said he believed he would go home, and several others decided to do the same. Two of the young men, Ansley Daniel and Parton David, asked Pastor Higgins if they couldn't go home and wait. At least they could be working a little, or helping put out the gardens, carrying cotton to be ginned, or selling vegetables in the market. Mr. Higgins smiled a little slyly and answered, "Yes, you can. You can all go home, but be sure to be back tomorrow. The missionaries arrive from Cape Town at the Luchenza station tomorrow afternoon. Your classes all begin next Monday in earnest."

We heard the loud babble of excited talk and wondered what in the world was going on. When recess time came, we surely found out. The teacher-training students and the evangelists were telling it everywhere. "*Adzafika m'mawa!*" they announced. "They are coming tomorrow!"

The mission had a motorcar and a lorry, both marvels to us. We saw the good Dr. Lee Rittenhouse and one of his nurses go to town every Tuesday to take care of patients in Limbe. We saw the lorry go, too, to get mission supplies.

This Friday a girl and I had gone to the hospital for something or other, and we saw Pastor and Mrs. Higgins drive away in the mission car. What was up? We asked one of the hospital boys, "Where are the Higginses going? Do you know?"

"The new missionaries are to come in at three," he answered. "The new ones who are to teach, you know."

We saw the Higginses' cook boy going up the diagonal road to the kitchen from one of the other mission homes. He had something in a basket. Maybe it was yeast, maybe cream, maybe a papaya or a pineapple. The houseboy was polishing the porch with red "*stoep* polish" for *Sabata*. The Afrikaans word for porch is *stoep*.

We went back to the *mpanda* to get ready for the opening of the Sabbath meeting. Everyone who was able to walk went to that meeting, the nicest of the week. The houses were clean, the church was clean, and lovely flowers adorned the pulpit. All, however poor, wore their best clothes. Food had been prepared, and no one at Malamulo went to market or mill or the garden on *Sabata*.

That evening we went to meeting earlier than usual, and our inspection of the *mpanda* was over quicker. We wanted to get a good glimpse of the newcomers. I sat in the choir in the front row. The pressure lanterns had been lighted and hung along the length of the grass-roofed church. They cast fitful, flickering shadows on the faces of the people assembled there. Friday-evening meetings were always homelike and informal.

Oh, dear, they were here—Pastor and Mrs. Lowell A. Edwards! How can I describe them? I don't know how to begin. I felt a strange, radiant warmth pass between Mrs. Edwards and me the moment our eyes met. It was as if I had been waiting for years for this moment. I can't explain it. It was almost holy, for the great God showed me in the smile she turned on me in that moment that He had not forgotten me or my sister or Camie.

I heard scarcely a word of the sermon. The new bwana, Pastor Edwards, offered prayer. It must have been strange to him to pray through an interpreter, for he was a bit halting. I half opened my eyes and looked at him. He had one of the kindest faces I had ever seen or ever will see. It was not hard to read what kind of missionary he would be.

How can I tell you about Dona Edwards? That smile she gave me was such as Lena, my Umame, often gave to me. It was as if she knew I would have a lot of little faults and failings, yet she would love me just the same. Her smile reminded me, too, of dear Father Akim. It was a sort of candle lighted back in the depths there, lighted, I knew, and burning for me.

All the while the pastor was talking, I was thinking strange new thoughts. It was as if I had been groping for years along a dark road. Suddenly a ray of light shone so entrancingly, I felt a surge of joy rush into my heart, and I began to stumble ahead, enraptured by the vision I had glimpsed. If you had walked in darkness and hopelessness as long as I, you would understand exactly how I felt. No hope, no light, no promise now or ever. Suddenly a light flickers up where you never dreamed a light would be.

I studied Pastor and Mrs. Edwards's faces the whole meeting through. I could not bear to take my eyes away for fear they would look at me again and I would miss that promise of precious things in those eyes.

"Did you see her smile?" several of the girls asked me back in our *mpanda* room.

"They look as if they will be kind," another one of my friends said.

Serapiah, my chum, accused me, "Alice, you stared at her the whole meeting through. You looked as if you would like to eat her up."

Then she laughed and added, "Don't do it. We have waited long enough for these teachers, and we need them badly!"

# 11.

THE great Malamulo Mission had been an estate where the owners attempted to grow coffee and fruit. They had sold the property to another organization, which in turn sold it to Seventh-day Adventist missionaries in 1902. The house where the new missionaries lived was built with the rooms in a long row like a train and had a kitchen like a crossbar on a T at the back. A *khonde,* or narrow porch, surrounded the house on three sides. Pretty vines grew on the porch, but I thought I should warn the Edwardses about that, for crawling snakes and lizards like to hide there.

By the side of the porch was the grave of little Jessie Ellingworth, a baby girl who had died in the early days of the mission. The mother, they said, was so frantic with grief she could not bear for them to take her baby to the cemetery on the hill. So they buried the child by the side of the *khonde.* I wondered if Dona Edwards would be afraid when she saw the little grave. I'd always felt a little slashing edge of fear when I'd passed it in the dark and had seen the tiny tombstone gleam in the moonlight.

In my plan for a happy life, a perfect life, the thing called death could come in and spoil every plan. I hated death.

Maybe Mrs. Ellingworth had been young like me. Maybe she thought she had a fine life with a good husband and a nice brick house and a baby girl. Then death and a little gravestone weighted her heart until it could never be light again.

One day soon after the Edwardses arrived, I saw Dona Edwards walking around the mission yard. She had on a pink dress, pretty and ruffly, with big white buttons. She did not know that over the hedge a pair of brown eyes watched her every step. She fascinated me. Was she happy? I wondered. She and the jolly bwana seemed to love each other very much. At church that last *Sabata,* we had seen him look at her from the pulpit and smile. She smiled back as if some kind of silent message went between them. Something like "I love you, dear. Always believe that."

I decided to walk slowly past the brick house to see if she would speak to me. I liked to hear her voice. I wondered why it stirred me so deeply, and suddenly I knew: It sounded so *very* much like my mother's voice when she would say, "Good morning, little Alice," or, "Come, let Mother button your dress, Mother's darling."

I tried to keep my eyes discreetly ahead as I walked past her house. I was looking, though, with my heart in my eyes. Oh, she had turned and was coming up the path toward me. My heart began to pound. She smiled and called me into her house.

Inside the Dona's house I looked around guardedly, and she saw my glance. "Our things are not here yet from America," she explained. "These things are not very pretty."

I thought they were lovely. The floor was polished and very clean. A vase of flowers graced the mantel. On the table sat a pressure lamp with a white shade. Through a doorway I saw a bed made smooth and neat, with fat pillows.

She wanted to know my name, and wanted to know if I spoke English.

"My name is Alice," I replied.

"You must help me with Cinyanja," she said. "I want to learn to speak the native language."

"The people will love that, Dona," I answered. "They love to have you speak to them in their own dialect. I will surely help you."

"Teach me a sentence now, Alice. Teach me to say, 'Good morning,' 'Good-bye,' and 'I believe it will rain today.'"

I was beside myself with joy. Here I was sitting beside her in her pretty living room. I taught her *moni,* a greeting for any time of the day or night. I taught her *Tsalani bwino,* our way of saying good-bye. Then I drilled her on *Ndikhulupirira kuti mbvula ibwera lero*—"I believe it will rain today." She made all kinds of cute, funny faces getting that mouthful out. To my amazement, she got it.

After a while she said, "I love pretty handkerchiefs, Alice, and I will give you two because I am so happy you helped me today. You can choose any ones you like." She held out to me a gold-colored box filled with dainty handkerchiefs.

I leaned over the box so she would not see my eyes, which were threatening to fill with tears. I was angry at myself. Why should I cry when my heart was going "ponk-ponk" with happiness?

I picked out one with a lace border, because she said she had crocheted it on the boat coming out to Africa. That made it doubly precious to me. I got another which I gave to my best girl friend. Before I left, she took my hand in her soft hands, and prayed for me. I'll never forget how she prayed that I would be a good girl, and that God would help me remember He had a special work for me to do.

After that I would maneuver to be "going her way" whenever I could. I'd carry her books or satchel, anything to be near her. I hung on every word she said and tried to imitate her way of talking and acting. She asked me about myself, my interests, my ambitions. Soon I was confiding in her my thoughts, feelings, and wildest hopes. I thought she was the one I had longed for with all my heart blood, but I was still not sure.

One day Mrs. Higgins told us that Mrs. Edwards was very sick with malaria. Suddenly the light seemed to leave the room. At mealtime I could hardly eat. Finally I went down to the hospital to see her. She had vomited all night, and her face was as white as marble. I was frightened. What if she should die? Someone said the Edwardses had two sons in America. What if their mother never returned to them? The thought of it gave me that old sinking feeling. I did not want anyone else to suffer as Tillie and I had suffered. Oh, dear, the world was full of trouble!

She told me she was glad to see me and reached out and patted my hand. I could see she had been crying.

She began to tell me about America. "I had a letter from home today," she said. "Our two sons, Robert and Charles, will graduate from college in June. We have looked forward to their graduation for a long time."

"And you won't get to be there, Dona?" I asked, with as much sympathy as I could put into my voice. (I was so overjoyed that the Edwardses were in Africa, I really couldn't make myself wish they were back in America. Already the teacher-training students were bragging about their fine teachers.)

"No," she answered, turning her head away a little, and I could see tears start in her eyes again. "No, and our oldest son Bob is married. There is to be a little grandchild in May."

"Oh, madam," I cried, clapping my hands. "You will want to knit that little babe a sweater and hat and some bootees. I will let you have some of my patterns. They are just lovely!"

Dona shook her head. "I can crochet, but I cannot knit, and I have no time. I am too busy teaching and running the house for Bwana. Can you knit?"

"Oh, yes, Dona, I can; and Mrs. Vixie has a lot of new lovely patterns. You get the wool and I will knit it for you. Oh, I will be so glad to do it for you!"

My fingers flew on the delicate wool Bwana brought from town. Every stitch was a pleasure. Now I was doing something for the love that bubbled up in my heart for dearest Dona. Her baby grandchild across the wide ocean would wear this sweater I was knitting!

Dona gave me ten shillings for knitting it, and I tried so hard to refuse. That was twice as much as I usually got for my knitting. I really did not want to take a thing.

"Take it, child," she said. "You need it. It is worth so much to me, a thousand times as much." She packed the little set with loving care and sent it off on the long journey to America.

The Higgins family left for America about this time, and Bwana Edwards was made mission director. He and Mrs. Edwards, who was well again from her malaria, moved into the house of the Bwana Principal on a hill.

I would climb that hill to get water any day rather than go to the river, which was nearer. Sometimes I saw her, sometimes I didn't. Often she would call me into the house. My heart would beat wildly with joy when she did that. Bwana was often there, smiling and happy over Dona's impulsive ways and proud of his clean, well-regulated, hospitable home.

"Why do you put branches in the waterpots when you have filled them with water?" she asked me once.

"It keeps the water from slopping out onto my head, madam," I laughed, wondering why she, wise as she was, would not know so simple a thing. "Don't you do it that way in your country?"

Then it was her turn to laugh. "I never saw anyone carry a waterpot on the head until I came to Africa."

That was a curious bit of knowledge to me. How did women in America manage to keep house without carrying a waterpot once in a while? Even in the native townships of Johannesburg they carried water, but in our hospital home we carried it from the faucet outside. In Sophiatown there was one faucet for many, many families. The mud was deep around it, and the women and girls had to wait in line. What kind of a place was America, where no one carried water?

I had heard a few fairy stories in the Johannesburg school. One was of an old Arab who rubbed a lamp and a fairy appeared to give him his heart's desire. I knew that no such lamp existed, yet in my girlish mind I toyed with every possibility. I decided to ask her a little about America every time I saw her. Of all fairylands, that one seemed the most fabulous. I had seen some pictures, too, that missionaries had shown me, of big houses with glass all around, cars, and all kinds of things I could not identify.

"Can hyenas and thieves and elephants break into those houses in America as they do in ours?" I once asked Mrs. Edwards cautiously. "And do wild pigs ever get into your gardens to tear them up? How do you keep the monkeys from eating up your maize?"

Dona's eyes danced, and I knew I had asked a funny question.

"There are no such beasts in America, except in cages to show people how they look," she told me. "Then there are performances called circuses where people can see the wild beasts." It was so mysterious to me, and strange; she even had to explain what a "cage" was. Dona Edwards did not think of me as ignorant, so I felt light and free around her. I learned not to fear to ask her anything.

There were things about my own body I wanted to know. I had been told that when terrible pains made me bend double I must hurry and marry, for it was babies scratching to be born. I was told also that during that time I must never touch salt. If I salted food, anyone, especially men, eating that food would surely get a deadly infection. I knew that Umame had salted food, but whenever I had used that argument, they answered heatedly, "She is dead, isn't she?" and, "Your father is dead, too." That reply had seemed so conclusive it used to scare me, but Tillie had scoffed and said it was not true. So I made up my mind to ask Dona about it. She would tell me.

In time I passed standard six and went into secondary school. I felt a little proud of my accomplishment. Students looked up to us, for few people were so fortunate as to get that far in school. And *girls* hardly ever got as far as standard five, much less standard seven or eight. I suppose I could be pardoned for being a little elated.

Ethel Msuseni and I were the only girls enrolled in the secondary school. I had gotten high averages in my standard six government examinations, and the names of the examinees and their rating were published in a small newspaper called *The African Weekly*. Another African paper, called *Msimbi* ("The Describer") also published the grades. These papers were read widely by the Africans, as they were so eager to climb out of the mud of ignorance.

After my grades were published, I began to get letters from all over south and central Africa. Educated girls were so scarce that young men in secondary schools everywhere wrote letters, proposing marriage to me. They had gotten a vision of what a home should be, and there were not enough educated girls to go around.

This gave the lie to what my people had always declared. They had violently opposed my going to school, lest I never catch a husband. They argued—reasonably they thought—that a man would not want an educated wife. This might be true of the old native African, but not of the emerging young African.

Dona jumped all over one of her students who once said he didn't want an educated wife. "Why?" she demanded.

"Because they *want* things," he answered lamely, looking at the floor. "And they become stubborn and talk back to their husbands."

"What things do they want?" she probed.

"Why, cups and plates and spoons and cloth for dresses," the student answered, so nervous by then that his pants legs were shaking.

"Don't *you* want cups and plates and spoons? Do you want your wife to go naked like a heathen?" Mrs. Edwards questioned.

Dona ran him into such a corner, he was sorry he had said a thing. She hung onto that subject like a dog shakes a rag. She helped students change many an attitude and discard many a superstition.

The smallest piece of Nyasaland paper money was a five-shilling note, worth about eighty-five cents. Five shillings was a lot of money to us students. I knitted many sweaters for less than that.

Imagine, then, my surprise when I began to receive letters containing these bills, which the senders called "tea money." "Here is a little tea money," a letter would say. "You do not even need to thank me. It is nothing."

I was in a quandary. I felt I should send the money back, yet I had no money to use for stamps. Besides, it was a temptation to keep the money; after all, I had not asked for it. Why should I spend my hard-earned pennies for stamps and paper to send it back? If they wanted to throw money away, why should I worry? So I soothed my conscience.

I wasn't earning much money at my part-time teaching work.

I had to knit every spare moment to keep even the simplest clothes on my back. I could not afford shoes, which were lovely things to be dreamed about in the misty future. If I had answered every letter, it would have taken every penny I could rake together.

But I had a feeling that something was not right. I couldn't ask Tillie, because she was teaching in Luwazi. If she had been nearer, I knew her gimlet eyes would have bored through me, and she would have been quick to tell me what to do. She would have punctuated her remarks by shaking her finger at me, and she might have finished with a few hard slaps, too. I've known her slaps to change my mind about several things.

What would Dona say? I thought I knew, and decided not to think about it right then. I was flattered, fearful, hopeful, and puzzled all at once. I had several pieces of the money under my clothes in my box of things. There was comforting security in having money. I cautiously cashed one note, bought stamps, and coyly thanked the donors. To my amazement, more little green five-shilling notes came. Eighty-five cents each!

My fingers ached with knitting and sewing all the time. My legs and back ached, too, from hard work. Now money was coming in continually, unasked for. I was getting along well in school, and I was being a little more clever than average in several things. I would have preened my feathers at the thought, if I'd had any to preen.

# 12.

ONE day Tillie sent word that she was being married to a man of Luwazi Mission, a good-looking teacher. She urged me to come home during the coming holidays so I could be present at her wedding. Of course I was eager to go, particularly since the Malamulo lorry was making a trip up to Mombera Mission, and I could ride that far free of charge. That meant that I would have to walk only 135 miles, and there were several of us going, so I would not need to be alone.

I was glad to get away from the scene of my new problems that weighed on my mind all the time. I hoped I might leave the feeling of guilt behind. I wished again and again I dared talk to Dona Edwards about it, but I was deathly afraid she would think I had asked for money and blame me.

I got my bundle of clothes ready, but did not take a bit of money. I put my box in the Domestic Building for safekeeping, as petty thieves were common everywhere, even on a mission station.

I found out it would be about an hour before the lorry started for Mombera. I would have time to go tell Dona Edwards, whom I had not seen for several days, good-bye. I did not want her to find out about that wretched "tea money" that was worrying the life out of me, but in just a short hour, she would not find out, I hoped. She would not have time.

"Odi!" I cried, approaching the house.

"Odini!" I heard her reply from the region of the kitchen.

I ran in there to find her. It was Tuesday—town day and no school at the mission. I was surprised to see Dona working in the kitchen. She was often at her typewriter or at her desk. She seldom had time for cooking, though she told me she loved to cook and work out new recipes.

"Where's Andy?" I asked, after greeting her. "He should be doing this work."

"He's sick with asthma," she answered, "and Wyson and Bwana have gone to town. With just me needing food, no sick cookboy is going to drag himself around and work."

I told her then about Tillie and her wedding. She asked me some things about Tillie, which I gladly told her.

Then her hazel eyes were full of interest. "I hope I get to see Tillie sometime," she said. "Is she like you?"

"No, she and Camie, my brother, look like our father. They tell me I look like our mother. But I don't really know. I can hardly remember them."

Then I told her about the mission lorry, and my chance to ride *almost* home, free.

"How far is 'almost'?" she asked.

My, she had a way of getting to the root of things! I began to get scared. Would she uncover my guilty little secret? If I stayed much longer, she would be sure to find out more than I wanted to tell.

"A hundred thirty-five miles," I answered in a low voice, not thinking of miles at that moment, but of little green five-shilling notes.

"*A hundred thirty-five miles!*" she repeated in a startled voice. "Do you mean, child, you'll walk that far? Why, that's terrible!"

"I have to," I answered, amazed at her solicitude. "That's the only way to get there. I've done it before," I added, hoping to comfort her. Yet I felt elated that she was so concerned about me. It was a delightful experience. My heart beat wildly as I looked at her dear face. She always told me she was not pretty, but I thought she was lovely, with those candles lighted in her eyes, and lighted for me.

"How long will it take you to get there, Alice, walking?" she queried.

"About three days, maybe a little more," I answered. "But we'll get to sleep at Mombera before we start; you know, we have a mission there. We may get there late at night—often we do—then only three days more and I will be home with Tillie!" I was eager to see Tillie; I had more to tell her than I'd ever had before in my life.

She kept asking me about the trip. Where would we sleep? Were there any wild beasts, dangerous men, dangerous places?

I hastened to explain: "There are houses, sort of 'rest houses,' built so we can sleep on the way there," I told her. "They are travel huts to camp in so we can be safe from wild beasts."

"What will you eat on the way? What do you have for a lunch on the way to this place you call Mombera?"

"Lunch?" I repeated, hardly understanding her. It was a word we did not use. I couldn't make out what she was trying to get at in this kitten-and-mouse question session. She was the kitten and I was the mouse. I wondered if she might suspect something and was trying to catch me, but that wasn't like her at all.

"I mean *food*," she said. "Have you food made up enough for your needs on the journey?"

"Why, no," I answered, mystified. What was she driving at, anyway? Everyone knew you just endured hunger on a long journey. Oh, some folks who had money had bought corn and sweet potatoes and would build a little fire and roast them. But I went hungry, and so did many others. That was one of the hardships we had learned to endure. It was a price we paid for travel.

"Do you mean you will go all day and all night for two or three days without food?" she asked. I had to laugh with pleasure at the look of sweet concern on her face.

"I ate a sweet potato and some *ntedza* this morning," I assured her. "Sometimes we find papayas or mangoes or guavas on the way, and the lorry driver stops if he sees a big tree. We're strong and young. It doesn't hurt us."

"But, Alice, darling, it hurts *me* to think of it," she said.

My heart did a double somersault again.

"When I get to Mombera Mission, I have friends there. The teachers will prepare us food. They always do. They are very kind," I said. "We will be all set for the trip on to Luwazi, so don't you worry about me, Dona."

When Dona learned we would be practically without food for three or four days of our journey, she fairly buzzed around the kitchen. "I won't have that, I won't have that!" she cried.

From her bread box she got fat loaves of brown bread, also sweet Malamulo butter from the wonderful paraffin (kerosene) refrigerator. She pressed a basket into my hand and told me to run to the hen house for eggs. These were to be boiled so we would have what she called "protein" to give us strength. Then I was dispatched after papayas from one of the trees, and big banana leaves to use for wrapping bread and the new thing she called "sandwiches"; the leaves, she said, would keep the sandwiches from drying up.

She made the most delicious sandwiches I ever tasted. I had not eaten a sandwich since dear Mother and Father had made some back in Johannesburg, when Tillie and I went on a church picnic. Dona found out that there were five of us, two boys and three girls, going, so she made fifteen sandwiches.

First she set me to buttering thirty slices of bread while she fried twelve eggs in her big iron skillet on the funny little Caledonia wood stove. I remember thinking, "It is just like the stove Mother had in Johannesburg." Then from the refrigerator she got some pickles and tomatoes, and she gave me salt in a little bottle. "When you eat this, put some pickle and onion with it," she told me.

She wrapped the sandwiches in banana leaves and then in newspapers, and put the lunch in a pillowcase from her dresser drawer. She cut several hands of ripe bananas from the *khonde*, and gave us all the sweetcakes she had, a whole dish of them.

"We don't need them," she laughed. "We're both too fat."

I would have wagged my tail if I had been a dog. I looked at her hands so busy for me, and felt a great desire to kiss them. Umame used to kiss us. Kisses meant love. Among most Africans little was known of kisses, only as they observed the custom among foreigners. But I remembered the thrill of Umame's warm, soft lips on my cheek and neck.

I did not kiss her hands; I was afraid to. I picked up the pillow-case, fat and ready to burst with goodies for us. I tried to stammer thanks, but I was afraid I'd burst out crying wildly if I said too much.

Then she did another wonderful thing. When she told me good-bye at the door, she pressed a yellow ten-shilling note into my hand. Speechless, I looked at it. This was not that nasty "tea money," but a love gift.

"This is to help take care of you," she told me, smiling again. I felt like throwing myself at her feet, and sobbing out all my worries and sorrows and getting her to help me solve them. This gift did more for me than blame and scolding would ever do. I stumbled from the porch with brimming eyes. As far as I could see her, she stood on the *khonde,* waving at me. "She doesn't know," I whispered to myself. "She doesn't know how bad I really am."

Now I knew I must be a good girl, for somebody cared whether I was hungry or tired, and I was sure now that she would feel hurt if I did wrong. It was like that song Bambo Richard Lumala taught us to sing in the church choir.

"I would be true, for there are those who trust me;
I would be pure, for there are those who care."

Yes, there were those who trusted me, and there were those who cared. At least, I could think of two people—Dona and Tillie. They were my little world.

We got on the back of the lorry and settled ourselves for the long, dusty, bumpy road. We loaded up in front of the doctor's house across the way from Dona's. We all waved at her when we left. It was ten o'clock when we left, and a little past noon when we decided to eat dinner. We had passed Blantyre and were traveling northward as fast as the age of the lorry and terrible state of the road allowed.

I shared my lunch with the other students. They, too, marveled as we ate those delicious sandwiches, and we all discussed Dona.

Her ears would have burned if she had heard me enlarging on her virtues, and I'm sure she would have laughed at my extravagant statements. My friends all agreed with me. Who wouldn't, when they were eating a lunch produced as if Dona, like Ali Baba, had rubbed a lamp for our special benefit?

We didn't get any farther than Lilongwe that night. It is a village of a few houses, a hotel, two or three stores, and a market. We stayed with some friends there.

I was all warmed with Dona's love and full of resolutions to be a good girl for her sake. But I found my friends at the village talking about a young man "very well educated," handsome and worldly-wise, who had been hired as an accountant in a tobacco company near there. They described in great detail his fine manners, his good clothes, and the high wages he was supposed to be earning. They also told me how handsome he was and what a "catch" he would be for some lucky girl.

"Even his tone of voice is different," one girl told me excitedly. "He can speak English, too. He uses scent, and he has a man-servant to work for him. He is for all the world like a big tea planter."

"What mission is he from?" I asked, innocently.

They laughed. "No mission, *nanunso*. He is an atheist; he doesn't believe in God at all. He laughs at churches and brags that they will never get any of *his* hard-earned money."

I shivered at the thought of an atheist. "He comes to dances," they said, "and makes the other young men mad with the airs he puts on before the girls. He is building a brick house, too."

I wanted to see this superior being with my own eyes. All of us longed for a better, more prosperous way of life; and when one of our number achieved it, we were more proud than envious. I was merely curious to see this lucky human being.

That evening, while several of us girls were taking a walk, I did see him. And my heart skipped a beat. To my amazement and secret pride, he stopped and looked past the other two girls right at—me. My heart began to thump clear up in my throat. I put my hand up there for fear he'd see it. I felt conscious of my patched dress and my bare feet.

"And who is the stranger?" he asked, in what I thought was a cultured voice. He held his head high, and I saw he carried a cane. Certainly I was impressed.

The girls tried to tell him, all talking at once. They were eager to show off to him that some of them were climbing up, too, and achieving something. "She's in the secondary school. Yes, she's had her name printed twice in the *African Weekly*," they boasted.

I only half heard their chatter, so magnetized was I by his handsome eyes, his high, intelligent forehead, and his flashing white teeth. Then suddenly I looked down at my bare feet. Prince charming was looking at me, and where were my glass slippers? For once I was speechless. That was strange, for Dona always said I chattered like a magpie. She talked a lot, too, so we were a team, really.

Before I knew it he had given the other girls money and sent them to the Lilongwe Mandala Store. They brought back sweet-cakes, biscuits, and big hands of fat bananas we loved.

He detained me. "Don't go—Alice. I want to talk to you!" he said in his low voice.

I was charmed as a bird is charmed by a rat or a snake. My young heart fluttered wildly. His white suit was neat and clean. His necktie was of silk. His white-and-brown shoes gleamed with polish. But while he talked, my mind kept returning to the fact that he did not believe in God. It was like walking on a blister or a cut place on your foot. I wished I didn't have to keep remembering the atheism.

Before the girls came back, he had told me so many flattering things I couldn't remember them all. "You're what I've been looking for all my life, *Ng'anga*," he said, calling me by one of the sweetest love names in our language. He began telling me all the things he would do for me when I would be his wife. There would be the servant to do the work, and I would have all the

dresses I wanted. There would be shoes for my feet and a wristwatch for my arm. My name was Princess? He'd see to it that I
would live like a princess, and it would be his pleasure to see me
dress like one!

We would be married as soon as he could get it arranged. He
learned the name of the *nkhoswe,* or marriage arranger, in my village. He said he'd go right away and make all the arrangements,
and he promised to write me and send tea money.

Tea money! By that time the girls were back, but those miser-
able words "tea money" sounded like an ugly toad croaking in a
forest where I had heard the *hlu-hlu* bird warble its sweet song.

I thought of my schoolwork, and I was shocked at the thought
of leaving it, never to finish—to marry a man who did not even
believe in God. Yet, I was enchanted by his persuasive manner
and personality. I was under a spell.

I had a hidden pocket in the yoke of my dress, where I had
secreted the ten-shilling note Dona had given me. We were still
eating of her bounty, and I felt as if I were betraying her when I
ate a frosted sweetcake this stranger provided. But it tasted lovely.
Everyone gets hungry for sweets, I suppose, and we girls used to
chew sugarcane to satisfy that hunger.

Funny how everything reminded me of things. Even while I
watched him pass out silver and heard a lot more rattling in his
pocket, I thought, "Pieces of silver—thirty pieces of silver."

I gasped at that. The price of the Lord!

Still I was charmed by his low, studied laugh, aimed at sound-
ing cultured; the gold ring on his finger; the wristwatch on his
arm; the plans he had whispered to me of a rosy future away from
the "pious missionaries, who never have a bit of fun."

I curled my toes in the red, crumbly clay, embarrassed. I dared
look up at him only briefly.

"You should have shoes, you know," he said smoothly. "Pretty
ones, red ones to wear with red silk dresses. You'd be fetching in
red. Has no one told you you're beautiful? White shoes, too, you
must have, so you can look like a princess."

He took off his watch and let me wear it for a few minutes on my slim arm.

"My wife will have a watch," he told me again, "only a small one, and she will have as many dresses as there are days in the month."

"My wife!" The caressing way he said that thrilled me as I had never been thrilled before.

"I'm in *love!*" I told myself that night as I lay on the bed mat beside Sarapiah, my friend. But the little bump that was the ten-shilling note pressed against my heart. I knew I was doing wrong. This was not the way Tata or Umame would have wanted me to go, and I knew Dona would be sad. She would go on working for people after I had done the things that pleased *me*. And Tillie —oh, dear! She would shake her finger so hard, and pinch! I would feel like running.

I held my destiny in my hands as I would hold a vase, filling it as I wished. What would I do now? I knew what I wanted to do desperately. I wanted to live in a brick house. I wanted as many dresses as there are days in the month! I wanted a wrist-watch to circle my slim arm, which he had told me was so pretty. I wanted white shoes, to be like a real princess, to queen it in the village, to dance, to skip, to be gay. He had lots of money; I heard it in his pocket! Crowns and florins and shillings, and I would have a purse with silver in it. Not pennies, but silver—"thirty pieces of silver"! Again I tried to shut out that thought. It made me angry to have it intruding all the time.

"I'll think about that later," I decided, "not now. I'm alone. Tillie is married now. I have no one. Surely it isn't wrong to do the best you can with your life. I have to work so hard to get one dress. Surely it isn't wrong to be happy!"

# 13.

WITH my conscience tugging from one side, dazzling dreams tugging from the other, and the feel of the bump against my heart besides, I got little sleep that night. When we started on the long walk the next afternoon between Mombera and Luwazi, I was tired and cross from the start. The journey had never seemed so long before. Hateful thoughts of rebellion and doubt, like black bats, flew around in my head.

"Why do you stay on with those silly missionaries?" he had sneered. "What have missionaries done for you? They're careful to see you don't climb too high. You've paid your way. You've worked hard. You owe them nothing."

I knew that I owed to the mission everything I had or was, but I did not want to admit it. I was such a coward. I should have told him about the pillowcase full of food, and the big fat sandwiches wrapped in banana leaves. I should have told him that Dona's hands flew like white birds to make me comfortable for my long journey. But I did not do it. I knew he would laugh and call me a sweet little thing, so easily deceived. He had been out in the big world and he knew!

I arrived in Luwazi too late for Tillie's wedding. There, night after night, the battle raged in my mind. Tillie, so dependable, so responsible, and so good, lay asleep in the next bedroom. What would *she* say if I told her of the terrible things I was thinking? I would not tell her, for a wicked daring possessed me. My life was my own to do as I wished. I wanted for once to decide for myself.

I saw my lover—shall I call him that?—again when I passed through Lilongwe. This time he took us through his new brick house, talking low to me and only me. When my girl friends would get out of earshot, he talked as fast as he could.

"I'll go to see your people," he whispered, "then I'll come get you—I'll get you away from those psalm-singing hypocrites, who shake hellfire and judgment in your face to scare you. They want you to be long-faced and ugly. They think even beautiful clothes are a sin. *Ng'anga,* I will get you away from it all.'"

I caught my breath as he spoke these last words. His voice went on and on, almost hypotizing me, compelling me to think his way. I felt like a little bird I once saw letting out little cries as it fluttered toward a big mamba snake that lay watching it.

Was Mrs. Vixie a psalm-singing hypocrite? No, never! She was so tender and kind, her voice low and gentle. And Dona? I thought of her busy hands buttering bread, wrapping sandwiches. I thought of the solicitude in her voice. A psalm-singing hypocrite? No, no! Was Bwana, so tender, so kind he was called *Wacifundo* (merciful one)? The lump that was ten shillings was a hard wedge now, breaking my hard heart. Tillie had given me food for my return journey, thus saving me from spending that ten-shilling note. I wished I would never have to spend it. I wanted to keep is as a talisman forever.

Back at Malamulo some tattlers got me into trouble about my tea money. I tried to explain, but they would not believe me. They thought I had written to boys asking for the money. Then, as if that weren't hard enough, when someone lost a ten-shilling note, my ten-shilling note was found with my five-shilling tea-money notes. It was such a mix-up. They were like dogs chasing a rabbit, and I was the rabbit.

I was tired and half sick from my journey. I felt guilty and cross. I decided not to fight. I had been fighting and scratching at life, but suddenly I decided to give up. I would get out of this mix-up somehow. Let them do to me as they pleased. What did I care? No use to tell of the splendid moments when I had decided to send back the money and start again. They would not believe me.

My heart was like a piece of stone in my breast. I quit reading my Bible. I quit praying. All God had done was to hurt me.

Right when I had decided to be a good girl, this had to happen.

They disciplined me with two weeks of hard work. They told me my mail would be read in my presence to shame me, before I would get to read it myself. I could not work anymore to earn a little money for my expenses. I could not sing in the choir, and that had been such a joy to me. I could not serve as one of the prefects in the compound to help advise and keep the girls in order. No one trusted me anymore. I had told some untrue stories in my frenzy at being in such a mix-up, for I was trying to cover up where the money had come from. But whose business was it anyway? I never asked for that money, and until now I had determined to restore it. Now, what was the use of anything? I was in trouble no matter what.

One thing bothered me. I had not been to see Dona Edwards since my return. That was bad manners, and I knew it. After all she had done for me, I had not been grateful. I had not greeted her and given her a *zikomo* (thank you), nor had I given her Tillie's *moni* (greeting) which she urged me to bring. Even by our Tumbuka standards this was very, very rude.

Tillie had never seen Dona, but she had been pleased and excited when I told her of my new friendship with the missionary lady.

"Sister! Sister!" Tillie had cried, her eyes sparkling—and she was clapping her hands, too—"Here is another answer to Tata's prayer. Oh, Alice, I can still hear that weak voice: 'God will send someone—someone—to take my place—*ng'anga!*' He said that, Sister. Oh, Sister, we are not forgotten! This Dona will love me. She will be a mother to me, too, and to Camie. Oh, God be praised!"

In the face of all this, I could hardly have told Tillie of this other—well—this tainted experience at Lilongwe. This longing for a few dresses, some shoes, and a wristwatch, and for the silly pleasure of queening it for a while. I felt like Judas's sister.

And that was not all I was doing. I was betraying this friendship with Dona, which Tillie said was from God. But I stubbornly refused to think of that side of it. My fabulous friend from Lilongwe was coming in all his splendor on Sunday, a little after the noon hour. I was to meet him at the "Come Again" gate. Of course it was all to be a secret.

I planned my route to "Come Again" so no one would see me. First I would get my box, made out of paraffin boxes. I would slip back of the *mpanda* to the waterside, past the dairy house, and through Dona's garden, where her garden boy, McFashion Nashion Nkosi, grew vegetables. From there I could see the *nkuku* house where I got eggs that day. Back of the Ansleys' mission house I would steal along until I got to where the trees grew thick, and then through the woods near the tree where two of the boys were killed by a bolt of lightning in a terrible storm a few weeks before. No one would see me, and soon I would be at "Come Again."

And I would be done with all this misery and injustice and disgrace. I would be through with Malamulo forever. And since the name Malamulo meant Ten Commandments, that could be taken two ways. I would be done with Richard Lumala, our kind choir leader, who could make his little choir sound like Miss Lydia Delhove's organ playing hymns at sunset. I would be done with Pastor Ivan Crowder's sermons that stirred my heart and made me want to live a better life. Done with Dona Vixie's helpfulness, Bwana Ansley's patience, Bwana Doctor's care, Dona Pierce's kindness. Done, too, with Bwana Edwards and the Dona who loved me like my own mother had. Suddenly I began to cry. I turned over on my little cot. The thick pad, to make it soft for me, was from Dona Edwards. "You need a mattress, dear," she had said. "My mother made this for me. My mother is eighty-four years old, and was not well when I left. I hope she will live till I get home, but I'm afraid she won't."

But when morning came, my rebellious feelings returned. I did my little chores around the *mpanda* with a strange feeling that I was standing off to one side watching myself. Tonight, I thought, when the girls gather for supper, I will not be here. They will ask about me. They will hunt for me. They will find me and my few patched old dresses gone. And the tea money, too! I will be on my way to my wristwatch, my white shoes, my brick house, my thirty dresses.

"And—your thirty pieces of silver," my silly conscience spoke out, "and the tree, too, where you will be hanged—you sister of Judas!"

Noon came. This was the last meal I would ever eat at Mala- mulo. The food was especially good that day; we had some ears of fresh maize. But I could hardly eat the food. I had two hours left. If I could only get the girls out of the house, I would pack my box. I was so nervous I wanted to scream.

At last the silly, gabbling things left me alone. I had less than an hour to pack and escape. I could not take everything. I would leave a note and give all I had left to Sarapiah. I was sitting on the floor there, sorting my little belongings for dear life. Then I stopped. The lacy, frilly thing lying there was the handkerchief Dona had given me that day. I dropped it as if it burned me. I could not take that. It was a part of my past life that I must forget.

Suddenly I became aware that someone was standing there in the doorway of the house. How long had Dona Edwards been standing there looking at me, looking my wicked soul through and through? I reached over and pulled my rough blanket over the box I was packing. What would have possessed her to come now of all times? I looked away, trying to harden my heart against this woman.

"Why, what's the matter, Alice?" That loving voice again. I wished I could forget it. Its cadences thrust like a sword into my soul. I tried to look as if nothing was going on, but I was trem- bling from head to foot. My hands shook like some old woman's. I wanted her to think I was just cleaning out my box and sorting things to make them tidy. What was wrong with that?

"N-nothing," I replied, not daring to look at her for fear I would burst out crying as I had the night before.

She came in, pulled up a chair, and sat down beside me. She laid her hand on my shoulder.

"What *is* the matter, Alice, dear?" She had not believed my other answer. Even a fool would have known I was lying, and Dona was not a fool. I wanted to run away.

"Nothing! Nothing! Nothing!" I almost screamed. Then something broke inside of me. I put my hands in front of my face and began to cry as hard as I ever had cried in my life. The great sobs came up out of my chest and tore at me till I could hardly get my breath.

Instantly Dona was on her knees beside me and had me in her loving arms. I could not help it, but I laid my head on her shoulder, and we both cried together. She was wiping her eyes with one handkerchief, and she found another, and was wiping my eyes, too. She talked all the time in her low voice, while the tears rained down her dear cheeks. How could she cry when she did not even know what was the matter? Could it be that she loved me this much?

"Tell me, dear. Tell me what we're crying about. I'm sure I can help you. I am strong. I know I can help you. See? I love you, Alice, dear. God sent me across the big ocean to help you. Love will find a way, Alice, dear. Bwana will help me, he is so good. We will help you, you darling!"

She leaned over and kissed me on the forehead. *Kissed* me, think of that! Wicked, ungrateful me; I had not been polite enough to take her Tillie's greeting. I burst out crying afresh.

The dirt floor of that *mpanda* hut was holy ground to me, for there I was converted. And conversion is a miracle. I wondered why I was ever tempted to sneak away to "Come Again." No longer did I care who waited at the gate. If the king stood there, it was nothing. I cared nothing for thirty dresses, or thirty wristwatches, or thirty pairs of shoes.

"Do you really, truly love me?" I asked, trying to still my trembling voice. I wanted to hear her say it again.

"Do you doubt me, Alice?" she asked quietly.

"No, no," I cried, "never, never, dear Dona. I have somebody now! Then I won't do it. I won't run away, I don't care how long he waits."

With the words tumbling out, I told her about it, feeling such a relief that I could hardly believe myself.

"I am glad you didn't sell Jesus for thirty dresses," she began.

"Nor for thirty pieces of silver, either," I declared, able to smile and laugh again.

"I'll tell you what," she said suddenly. "Come up the hill and be my girl. We need you, and you need us. We left our other children overseas. We need a child. Come on, dear. You're ours from now on. We'll fight these battles out together, you sweet child."

The pretty room she prepared for me had white sheets, a pillow, a fluffy blanket, and a pink bedspread. I had a dresser, too, the first one since my own Umame had died, and a crocheted rug in front of my bed.

A mother could not have treated me kinder. A father could not have been more considerate and thoughtful than Pastor Lowell Edwards. Now I had such a security as I had not dreamed possible, and the sweet pleasure of being included and loved.

# 14.

WHEN Christmas came, the Edwardses had a tree and made a party for all the mission children. After they were gone I helped Dona clean up things. She and Pastor Edwards gave me my gifts. I had my first nylon petticoat, and she got pink cloth for a dress for me. Bwana gave me a pound note. I could have wept for joy. I looked at my things many times a day and could hardly wait for Tillie to see my new home. I had written her jubilantly of my good fortune.

Dona said we ought to send a little joy to Tillie, so we made up a box for her. Dona got dresses and petticoats out of her own wardrobe, and two lovely handkerchiefs. She packed a comb, a pair of scissors, a tin of peach jam, a piece of cloth, and a sweater. I could almost see Tillie running and jumping for the joy and wonder of it.

Sitting in my pretty room, with my own brass kerosene lamp gleaming on my study table, I wondered how I could have dreamed of running away. I could look out of my window and see the dreary procession of poor and sick on their way here, there, or nowhere. Now God had answered Tata's and Tillie's prayers for me, and had saved me from a fearful trap from which I could never have extricated myself.

"Do not be contented with less than your very best," Dona used to tell me. "If you are only setting a patch or making an apron, do it as beautifully as you can. Every act and thought of your life is you. It is your character you are making—not patches and aprons."

One of Dona's friends in America sent me the prettiest clothes I had ever dreamed of—pleated skirts, gay sweaters, frilly blouses, and dainty underclothes. I could hardly believe that the girl I looked at in the mirror was *me*, Alice Princess Msumba. But it was. All I lacked were the glass slippers. I had no good shoes, for none could be found for my feet. Dona's shoes were too large, or she would have shared them with me, as she did everything else.

I did not mind. Few of the other girls, or boys either, had shoes. Most imported items were not getting through in those years after World War II, and the little that came through was expensive. Dona bought many a piece of cloth for needy people about that time, when cloth was so scarce and expensive. Looking at my pretty wardrobe, I knew I had better things than I could have ever gotten by running away. God was far better to me than the devil had promised to be.

Dona taught me to be unselfish. Every day of my life she counseled me kindly. Of course there were some people who went around saying that Dona would spoil me, but they didn't know what they were talking about. Dona loved me too much to spoil me. And how she would snort and cavort in class when she lectured on child care. She almost scared the mothers out of their wits. She taught that giving in to their children all the time and letting them do as they pleased was closing the very doors of heaven to them.

A lovely skirt came in one of the boxes she got for me. It was red, with a border of white flowers like camellias, I think, all around the edge. I jumped up and down with joy. The blouse, matching it, was white trimmed in red. It was gorgeous. No cloth in any Mandala or Limbe Trading or Kirkaldy Store was as lovely as this!

Dona watched my joy smilingly. Then she spoke quietly: "Now, you go pick out one of your other skirts and blouses and give it to the poorest girl in the *mpanda.*"

I stared at her. Surely she could not mean it. Every garment I had was associated with some little happy experience Dona called "thumbmarks." I didn't want to give up a single one. My face must have had some stubborn lines in it; for she continued, "One of the loveliest of the Christian graces is being mindful of others. Generosity is greatly rewarding. One of the ugliest things in anyone's life is selfishness. In your joy in getting pretty things, you must learn to share, Alice, with girls who get discouraged and sad wearing old things. Loving others is the basis of all Christianity. You must do this from real joy, not just duty."

Then she read to me the thirteenth chapter of First Corinthians. The way she explained it, I could see the philosophy that ruled her and Bwana's lives.

They didn't just preach unselfishness, either. One evening somebody told Dona that a woman at the hospital had pneumonia, and had no blanket.

"I'll find you a blanket," Dona offered.

I stopped her in the hall. "Dona," I whispered, "where are you going to get that blanket? You gave a blanket to McFashion Nashion, one to Pastor Malinki, and one to Sibande. You do not have any extra ones!"

"The woman is cold and sick, and needs a blanket," she answered me shortly. "I'm getting one off the guest-room bed."

I hurried after her. I knew she did not have even *one* to spare. She had just exactly enough for her beds. If she gave away the one off the guest-room bed, what would she do if someone came? And someone was always coming to her house.

She went ahead and peeled the blanket right off the bed, leaving the sheets.

"Dona," I said, "what will you do if someone comes tomorrow? I know you have faith, but God would have to throw a blanket right down out of heaven if a guest comes."

She laughed, and headed up the hall with that blanket. She paused at the parlor door.

"Listen to me, Alice," she said, patting me on the cheek. "I could not be so cruel as to have a blanket lying idle tonight with some poor soul cold these long hours. I could not sleep or live with my conscience if I did that. She might die, and her death could be my fault. God's arm isn't shortened, my dear. He has never failed me yet."

Tillie came up that spring with her baby boy, and visited with me in my pretty room. She was amazed at Dona. Nothing like this had ever happened to us. She was just as kind to Tillie as to me. She gave her dresses and petticoats and hankies and night-gowns. My sister was amazed.

"God did this for you, Sister," Tillie said, her voice low with emotion. Then as usual my wonderful big sister had wise counsel for me: "For all these things, God will require more of you. Do not forget that. 'To whom much is given, much is required!' That is in the Bible. We cannot see the future, but God has something very special for you. I really believe this, Alice."

My lessons were coming along wonderfully. I was taking standard seven. I was secretly a little gratified, too, for few girls ever got through even standard five. I had algebra, geometry, history, advanced English, English literature, chemistry, physics, biology, advanced domestic science, and of course, religion. Pastor Edwards taught most of our classes. Mrs. Grace Stevenson, a wonderful missionary lady, taught us English. It was hard work, but a lot of fun.

The most exciting thing happened then. Four years had gone by, and Dona and Bwana were going to Cape Town for what missionaries call a "coastal furlough," and I was to go along. Just think! I, who had never seen South Africa since that terrible journey with dear Tata, was going to see Johannesburg again, and Barberton, and we would live several months in Cape Town. I had read of this great seaport, and now I would see it with my own eyes! Dona told me so.

Before Dona got all her things packed, she came home from Blantyre one day all excited. She ran in the front door while Bwana was still turning into the driveway. "Alice! Alice!" she cried. *"Mphatso yanu!"* ("Gift for you!") She loved to talk Cinyanja.

She had a white box under her arm, and her eyes were dancing. *"Mphatso!"* she cried again, and shoved the box into my hands. In it was a gorgeous pair of white slippers, dainty and lovely enough for a princess!

She stood there, her eyes dancing with the joy of making *me*
happy. She had no shoes as pretty as these, her own self.

Dona was unpredictable, and she always said I was, too. She
said she never knew what I would do next. Bwana often said it
was a nerve strain to have two tornadoes in the house at once. Then
he would laugh his delightful laugh. I guess I acted "unpredictable" when I saw those shoes. I gave Dona one look, then ran to
the door at the end of the hall. There were three or four girls out
in the road, on their way to Mwalamphanda.

*"Inu,"* I shouted, *"bwerani, bwerani!"*

They dropped what they were doing, wiped their feet on the
grass, and came on the run to Dona's porch. I let them into the
hallway and led them to the table where my lovely shoes were
sitting like jewels in a jewel box.

"We must thank this madam," I whispered. "Let's pick her up
and carry her. Let's make a little song. Let's say, 'Thank you, God,
for sending a mother to Africa.' "

They nodded. We knew our tunes. We had tunes for pounding, tunes for making brick, tunes for chopping. We knew.

They stood around the table, while I made a flowery speech.
I explained that these were the first expensive and proper shoes
I had ever owned since my other mother, now long dead, had
bought shoes for my little-child feet.

Then suddenly we swooped under Mrs. Edwards and lifted her
high in the air. I could hardly sing for laughing at the absolute
amazement on her face.

*"Zikomo mulungu,"* we sang. *"Upatsa amai kwa Africa!"*

Oh, my pretty shoes. They seemed too lovely for just feet. I
felt like wearing them on my head!

# 15.

BWANA and Dona ordered a new car from America, a Chevrolet. I was immeasurably excited and proud. An automobile in *my* family!

Finally their car came. We packed it with our things and started on the long journey to Cape Town. I was never more excited in my life. What I did not know was that they were planning to hunt up my relatives—cousins of my mother in the town of Barberton, east of Johannesburg. One of these cousins, Miriam, had come to our house after Mother had died, and pleaded with my father to let her have me. Tata looked down at my little face, so much like Mother's face, and said he could not bear to let me go.

"No, no," he cried, his voice breaking with sobs. "My wife is gone. I can't lose my children, too! Don't speak of it again."

Miriam cried and took me on her lap. She looked so much like my mother that I clung to her. But I did not want to lose my Tata.

Of all my relatives, Miriam seemed to be the nearest. She had kept in touch with us a little through Mrs. Davy at Luwazi, but since Tillie and I were not used to writing letters we had not heard from her for a long time.

The jacarandas, lovely trees with purple flowers, were in full bloom when we came near to Barberton, east of Johannesburg. There must have been hundreds of the trees, filled with bright mauve blossoms. The city lying in the valley below us seemed laced with lavender. We stopped the car and feasted our eyes.

At the edge of town the Edwardses rented a "rondavel," or thatched house, for the weekend. It is round like a Zulu hut, but with a neat cement floor and furnished with cots. Tourists bring their own bedding. As soon as we got all the things lugged in, they went out to the car again. "Come on," they told me. "We're going out to get food and also hunt up Miriam, your cousin."

We went to the Barberton hospital first, for Miriam was a nurse just as my mother had been. Inquiring at the desk, we learned she was in the out-patient section, a group of small houses where the patients sort of camp out while they are having treatments. It is a merciful arrangement so that the poor can get help.

Miriam must have been well thought of, for the white lady at the desk asked, "Is she a relative of yours?"

"She is a cousin," I answered proudly.

The lady looked me up and down. "If you are in the mood for taking the nurses' course," she said, "we would like to have you. If you are anything like Miriam you would always have a job."

Dona and I left Bwana reading in the car and walked down a long lane, as we were directed, toward the little out-patient village.

Dona knocked at the door of a building labeled "office."

A handsome woman, with a smooth brown face and lovely eyes, came to the door. Her uniform was spotlessly clean. She wore a filmy white veil on her hair and down her back just as I remembered seeing my mother wear. That is part of a nurse's uniform in Africa.

When she learned I was "little Alice," Lena and Akim's little girl, she threw her arms around me, weeping out loud with joy. Then she met Dona, and they became friends at once. Dona let me go home with Miriam for the weekend.

It was like heaven to be with Miriam, but when that Chevrolet drove up in front of Miriam's house to take me to church Sabbath morning, I could have wept for joy, for I had spent a whole night away from dear Dona and Bwana. Miriam was a little disappointed that I would not settle down to stay with her and her husband, Mr. Ben Nkosi; but Dona and Bwana had captivated me, heart, soul, and body, and it would kill me to lose them.

When Tillie and I were little, and Mother was on day shift at City Deep, we would go out in front of our house and strain our eyes toward the hospital. We would see other nurses come and go. Suddenly *she* would turn a corner and start toward us. So special, so precious, we jumped up and down in ecstasy. Mother was coming! Mother meant everything: clean house, clean beds, clean clothes, clean hearts.

Dona and Bwana gave me that same feeling. They took all my worries on top of theirs, and they had plenty of their own.

On Sabbath, for my sake, I knew, they hunted up the colored church. The Sabbath school superintendent, an Asian Indian, was all smiles as he welcomed "visitors from a far country" with deep courtesy. He asked Dona to sing for them.

Now, Dona doesn't like to sing. She would much rather tell stories, but she never refused any reasonable request. "Let Alice and me sing a duet," she said.

She and I had practiced *"Pakuitana Mbuye wanga,"* ("When the Roll Is Called Up Yonder") in Cinyanja many times. I sang the alto and she sang the soprano. The people liked the song so well that they asked us to sing the same song for the church service.

The audience was about half Indian, half African. Some of the Indians invited us home for dinner. Dona and Bwana loved all kinds of people and experiences, so they were glad to go. A great table was set in the living room, and Dona, Bwana, and I were given places of honor.

The house was big and rambling and furnished with sets of rooms for the married sons who lived together with the parents. The daughters-in-law and the little cousins were all there, like a big happy family.

Arriving in Cape Town, I got my first glimpse of the great salt sea I had heard so much about. The first thing I did was to kick off my slippers and run out into it and taste it. "It is salty," I cried. "It is!"

They got a pretty house in Claremont, called "Lothian." It had a yard and three bedrooms and two baths. It was furnished, and was cool and comfortable.

We had no sooner moved in than Dona and Bwana wanted to look up a man they called Pastor Cardey. He was in charge of a religious broadcast called "The Voice of Prophecy," with offices in the basement of a church near the Duncan Docks. In connection with the broadcast, he managed a small printshop.

When we drove up, Pastor Cardey happened to be out in front, and he came over to the car immediately, smiling. You could tell he thought a great deal of the Edwards family. As they talked, I just sat in the back seat, knitting a scarf or something.

I heard him talking in a low voice to Dona, and I noticed he kept looking at me. She shook her head and protested violently to him about something. Bwana was laughing and talking to another acquaintance who had come along.

Suddenly Dona turned around and introduced me to Pastor Cardey. She was a little disturbed about something, for her lips were in a thin line, and there was a little dent in one side of her chin. It always appeared when she was displeased. Bwana called it "the hole in her chin." He'd say, "Something wrong, Mamma? There is a hole in your chin." Then she would laugh and the hole would disappear.

Back at Claremont, as we were getting supper, she told me what had happened. "I wish people would stop trying to be so *helpful!*" she exclaimed. "He's got some fellow there in his printshop who wants to marry you. He says you'd be a perfect couple."

"Ha!" I hooted. "I want no Cape Town husband. I would never, never want to live in Cape Town."

"He is from Qumbu," she said. "He is from the Xhosa tribe, the same tribe as your mother. When Pastor Cardey found that out, he was determined for that fellow to see you."

"Well, I don't want to see him," I answered. "I'm perfectly satisfied. I shudder at the thought of getting married."

"You mustn't feel that way, Alice," Dona said. "See, I have a happy home and a pleasant life. Somewhere there is someone who will help you make a home which will be a little heaven. We will pray that the Lord will lead you to just the right person."

Later on she told me that Pastor Cardey had invited the three of us to an anniversary party for the Voice of Prophecy on Thursday night. They were going to have a program and ice cream and cake. He said it would be a good chance for this young man, Hulme, as he called him, to meet me. I did not want to go.

"Well, we just won't go, then," she answered. "I'm not going to force you into any situation you would not enjoy."

Pastor Cardey was a little perturbed because we did not plan to go, and he called us up on the telephone. Dona told him I really did not want to go, and that was true.

But the pastor insisted: "I have a moving picture I'm sure you'd like to see. I will show it to you at my house. Then we're going to a nearby town, where I want to show a temperance moving picture. Bring Alice. I would like them to see each other, at any rate. My boy is just as good as your girl," he teased.

"Oh, do you think so?" laughed Dona.

Dona told me all about the conversation, and I was amused.

"I'm happy, Dona, just staying with you and Bwana," I told her. "I've been bargained for and *lobola*-ed so much that I'm sick of the thought of marriage. You've saved me much sorrow and misery. I'd rather be *mbeta* [unmarried]."

"Well, let's not say that, but we do have a kind invitation, and just meeting this young man doesn't mean you have to marry him," Dona reminded me.

We went Thursday night to the pastor's house. Just as we arrived, Pastor Cardey and his protégé came down the street. The minister's eyes sparkled with fun.

"Hulme," he said, "this is Alice, Mrs. Edwards's girl, of whom I told you. Alice, this is Hulme Siwundhla, who takes care of the printing of our lessons at the Voice of Prophecy. Mrs. Edwards told me your mother was of the Xhosa tribe. Hulme is from that tribe, too."

I soberly shook hands with this man. I noted his clear, honest brown eyes, frank, intelligent face, his neatness and quiet good taste.

The moving picture we saw that night told the story of Stephen Foster and how strong drink destroyed him.

Before we parted that evening Hulme came and sat next to me and said softly, "When they sang 'I Dream of Jeanie With the Light Brown Hair' in the picture, I couldn't help thinking, 'Alice with the dark brown hair.' I have been praying for God to help me meet a well-educated, refined Christian girl. Maybe you are the one. I believe you are!"

"Oh, I'm quite sure I'm not," I protested. "You see, my home is very far away. That makes it impossible for such a thing to be."

"I wouldn't say so," he answered. "Do not fill your heart and mind with prejudices, Alice, but pray about this. I, too, will pray. Good night, Alice."

When I was getting ready to go to my room that night, Dona stopped me.

"Bwana and I both feel strange about this young man, Alice. We feel that he is good and refined and intelligent, as the pastor said. Pray about this, for we must not run before the Lord. The ways of God are 'past finding out.' "

"Why, he said that, too!" I exclaimed in great surprise. "What shall I pray for, Dona?"

"Only for guidance, my dear. Only that God will lead you. Let us not make any effort to further this thing at all. Let us just let God lead out."

"All right, Dona," I replied. "Good night."

"Good night, Alice."

Dona and Bwana went out of their way to make things especially pleasant for me. They heard that the Wynberg colored church was presenting a Christmas program in the Wynberg Town Hall. They knew I had never seen a nativity play, and they wanted to take me.

The young people were raising money for some purpose, I forget just what, and I think it cost a shilling to get in to see the play. We got seats up near the front of the crowded hall. The lights were dimmed, and shepherds were sitting on what looked like a grassy pasture. A bright star flashed out in the rafters above the stage. What looked like a group of real angels came in, and the song they sang sounded heavenly to me. They were dressed in white, and had shiny stuff on their hair and wings. It was so wonderful, I reached over and squeezed Dona's hand.

We saw the manger, the babe, and the wise men with rich gifts. Then the curtain rolled down. An announcer indicated the first half was over, and there was to be an intermission.

Right away I felt thirsty and thought of the big thermos jug in the car across the street. Dona said, "Wait a minute, Alice, and I'll go with you."

I wasn't irritated at her, but I was a little bit amused. What could hurt me? My face must have shown what I was thinking, for she said, "Now, you wait, dear. I *must* go with you."

In spite of Dona's warning, I ran ahead of her. She was coming down the steps just as I stepped into the street.

Suddenly a rough, dirty hand clamped itself over my mouth, and another hand was choking me. I was being half carried, half dragged down that dark street. I couldn't even scream.

I struggled, kicked, scratched, and tried to bite the hand that pressed against my mouth. Those seconds seemed hours long, but then I heard Dona coming, and I mean I *heard* her. She was screaming so, I wonder that folks down at the docks several miles away did not hear her. Maybe they did.

"Get your dirty hands off my girl!" she shouted. The next thing I knew, my captor let go my mouth to ward off a blow she had aimed at his head with her fist. My! She looked fierce. Her eyes blazed.

"You dirty scollies," she screamed, lashing out at them. Like a leopard fighting for her kitten, she scratched and tore. The men both let go of me and started to run. I heard their heavy shoes clumping away.

Trembling violently, I ran to Dona and threw myself into her arms. Dona hardly saw me, for looking malevolently at my fleeing assailants. Even in that terrible moment a warm feeling stole over me, for someone loved me enough to risk death for my sake!

I couldn't help thinking about Hulme sometimes, and when I

did, my heart did a double flip-flop. Hulme was mannerly and well
educated. He was a friend I could be proud of, and he was far
more handsome than the Lilongwe man. When I asked Dona
what to do, she said, "Alice, do as your little heart tells you to do
this time."

I was surprised, for she was always warning me about dangers
here and there. This time she left it all to me. She must have
thought he was all right or she would have gotten that hole in her
chin and gone after me hammer and tongs.

Dona's mind hopped around like the *kalulu,* as we called the
hare. You never knew just what she was going to say or do next.
Once, out of a clear sky, she said, "Alice, I have a strange feeling
about that young man, Hulme. I've tried to dismiss him from
my mind. I don't want you to live in Cape Town; I don't see
any future for you here. Yet I cannot get that fellow out of my
mind!"

"What do you mean, Dona?" I asked, watching her face
almost fearfully.

She looked at me a moment, and I thought she looked a little
puzzled. This was strange, for she was usually quite sure of her
opinions and not afraid to declare them.

"I hardly know," she said, slowly. "He does sum up to all that
I had hoped your husband someday would be. He is educated,
ambitious, polite, good-mannered, good-looking, and he loves God.
Not only that," she added. "He is a Xhosa, the same tribe as your
mother was. He came from the same place where your mother
and her people lived. It seems more than a coincidence."

"But how could I marry him, Dona?" I cried out fearfully.
"He is a South African. I don't want ever to live down here! I'll
never forget those terrible scollies! This city makes me afraid!"

Bwana would read of assaults, attacks, and uprisings that made
me scared to poke my nose out of doors. I think they were glad to
put a little caution into me.

"All big cities are dangerous," Bwana told me once when I was
expressing my fears. "San Francisco has its crime; so have Chicago

Rondavels of the Xhosa people in Bechuanaland. Alice's mother
was a Xhosa, as were both parents of Hulme Siwundhla.

and New York. One of the cabin boys on our boat told us he was
almost killed in Shanghai. Cape Town is not the only wicked
city in this world."

"But I don't want to live here!" I cried. "I like the quiet of the
bush country, the water of the lake, the flowers in the woods,
the—"

"Malaria, the leprosy, the dysentery, the bilharzia," interrupted
Bwana, a smile on his face. "There is evil in every place, Alice.
You can't escape it. But I don't like the city, either. Dona and I
like the bush country best."

"If I married Hulme, I might have to live *here*," I said, almost
crying.

Dona patted my shoulder and laughed. "I don't blame you a
bit," she said. "But, child, never limit the power of God. If He
has it in His plan for you to marry Hulme, He can move mountains
and bring miracles to pass. You cannot see ahead, child. You must
learn to trust."

79

# 16.

ONE Sunday afternoon Dona came into the dining room where I had my school books spread out to study. It was hot and muggy. My head ached from much application.

"Leave your geometry and English and history, dear," she said. "Let's go take a walk. I've worked at my desk till I have cobwebs in my mind, and you must have a few of them, too. Let's go get some fresh air. Bwana is asleep, and a brisk walk will do us both good."

I ran and changed my dress and washed my face and smoothed my hair. Soon we were headed toward the Claremont business district. It was funny. Every time Dona and I went for a walk, big, tall Zulu or Basuto fellows would call out saucily to me *"Uhamba namalungu zonke isikhathi?"* "Why do you go walking with your white madam? Why can't you go out alone sometime?"

Dona understood enough of what they were saying to me, surprisingly enough. She would smile and say, "They just don't know, do they, that you're not a prisoner. We are happy together."

We loved to window-shop, gawking at the pretty things draped around in the store windows. The *ticky* bazaars were the nicest of all. We went down one side of the main street of Claremont, taking in every store, down to where the Cape Colored folk sell flowers. Then across the street, taking in the stores on the other side, laughing and discussing the displays.

Suddenly a man was standing beside us, and we looked up. It was Hulme, the young man that Pastor Cardey thought so much of. In spite of myself, my heart began to pound.

"Good afternoon," he said pleasantly.

Dona greeted him kindly.

"Madam," he said hesitantly, "I have been wanting to ask you if you would come and talk to the Langa Church. That is the church where I belong. The pastor told me this week please to ask you. We have heard that you go and talk and tell stories in all the Cape Field churches. We would like to hear some of the mission stories, please."

Dona promised to oblige as soon as her schedule permitted.

I hoped that Hulme would not notice how fluttery and self-conscious I felt inside. I looked down to see if my heart was making my blouse flutter. He asked Dona if he might walk home with us so he could see where we lived. She laughingly consented, and he walked by my side all the way to our house.

When we crossed the street, he put his hand under my elbow to help me. It was such a far cry from the way girls and women were treated in my own country up near the equator, that I could not help being pleased. The men there never dreamed of helping the girl. Indeed, *she* was expected to carry *his* load. He always walked in advance of her, and she came struggling along, with heavy bundles in her hands and on her head.

When we got to our house, Dona suggested I take him to the dining room while she got supper. When I went to help her, she told me to make Hulme some cold lemonade. We visited for a little while, but as it was getting late, he left. From the satisfied look on his face, I knew in my heart he was glad he had found out where we lived. I felt sure we would see him again.

I guess I dared to daydream a little after that. Who could help it? I had never really been in love before, so I did not recognize the strange, sweet emotions that were playing hide and seek with my heart those days. Every word he had said to me came back in sweet clarity while I helped Dona with the housework and the cooking. He even intruded into my studies.

On Wednesday of that same week he called by telephone to ask if Dona would allow him to take me to prayer meeting in Plumstead. Dona told him it was all right if I wanted to go, but we must watch out for the scallies. She handed the phone to me, and I talked to him over the wire for the first time.

I was more than glad to go. It got to be just wonderful to hear the doorbell, and to know that *he* was there at the door. I began to understand what Dona had meant when she told me of true love. She used to say that it is the loveliest thing in the world when consecrated by the love of God. She told me that Bwana was the most precious person in the world to her. Now I could see why she had protested so vehemently against my affair with that fellow I had been so enamored with several years before. She told me I was wasting my youth and losing out on the sweetest thing of life. "Good things are always worth waiting for," she said. "You will have more preparation if you wait, and more love, too, of the right kind."

When Hulme came to visit, he always had a strange procedure. As soon as we were together, he would say, "Let us pray, Alice, and thank the dear Lord for allowing us to meet each other."

This night, after his prayer, he sat there talking in his low voice. Then suddenly he reached out and took my hand in his. My heart did a double somersault.

"Alice," he said, "I told you before about my prayer for a wife, and about the remarkable dream I had. I am sure—yes, I'm more sure every day that *you* are the answer to my prayers."

I was all atremble inside, for what girl could resist such a romantic situation? I had been dreamed about before he knew I existed.

"Alice," Hulme continued, "I have decided to ask you to marry me. I don't know how this can come to pass, and how all the difficulties can be overcome, but the same Lord who gave me the dream can help me. He has a thousand ways."

"Why, Hulme, Dona and Bwana are always saying that!" I interrupted him, excitedly.

"Have they told you that, too?" He smiled, and took my other hand. "They are more than a father and mother to you."

He hesitated a moment, then went on: "Alice, dear, will you marry me? Will you be my wife? I will work for you all my life, if you will! All that I have will be yours!"

"Wait just a moment," I cried, jumping up and pulling my hands away from him. "I'll have to go ask Dona. I couldn't promise a single thing without asking her."

I was out of the dining room in a flash and down the hall to the bedroom. "Dona! Dona!" I cried.

When she called out, "Come in," I ran in and threw myself down on a chair by her side.

"Dona— he wants— to marry me. He asked me to marry— him. He said, 'Will you be my wife?' I told him I'd better ask you and see what you think about it. That's a big decision to make all by myself. I'm afraid."

Dona was laughing so hard that the tears stood in her eyes. I didn't see one funny thing about it, but I guess she did.

"Oh, Alice," she said, "that is one question you'll have to answer for yourself. I can't answer it for you. You must ask your heart if you love him enough to love him forever."

"I already asked my heart," I answered indignantly, "and it answered Yes. But I asked my head the same question, and it answered No. My head said this cannot be! There are too many things in the way! Oh, Dona, what can I do?" I burst into a flood of tears and threw myself into her arms for comfort.

In a little while I went back to my lover and told him I would marry him if God would make clear the way. As for me, I did not see how it could be, but Dona said God could do anything.

"I say the same thing, too," Hulme said in his quiet way. "Oh, Alice, dear, I love you as I never dreamed it would be possible to love anyone."

Then he reached down in his pocket and brought out a dainty jeweler's box and laid it in my hand. I opened it cautiously, my heart too full of wonder for words.

There lay a perfect little gem of a watch, as lovely as any I had ever seen. My hands were trembling so that I could not get it out, but he did, and put it on my arm. "A seal of my love, dear," he said, and he put his arms around me and kissed me. I jumped up then, and we both showed Dona the lovely watch.

# 17.

BEFORE we left Cape Town, Hulme took me to the zoo, where for the first time I saw lions and leopards behind bars. I had certainly seen enough of them out in the bush scratching at our frail doors at night.

Then he introduced me to ice cream and ice-cream sandwiches, which I did not like so well at first. They were so cold they gave me a headache.

He found out from Dona that I had never had a new purse, so he bought me a lovely white one. It had so many compartments that Bwana laughed and said it was equipped with a parlor, bedroom, and sink. I did not know just what he meant by that. Hulme had bought all kinds of little things and filled it full—hairpins, bobby pins, a comb, a set of side combs with rhinestones, two pretty brooches, a box of powder, a bottle of perfume, hand lotion, cold cream, and a tiny pair of scissors. I squealed and laughed all the time I was unpacking the purse. The others laughed with me.

At last the day came when we had to leave for Nyasaland, and I had to bid Hulme good-bye. Before long, 3,000 miles of bushveld, plains, and mountains would separate us.

He came to see me the night we were packing, and we both shed tears. We knew that it would be months, maybe years, before we would see each other again.

We started back through East Griqualand. On the way we stopped at Qumbu to see Hulme's mother. She was a lovely, kind lady, and Dona was well pleased with her.

Bwana kept complaining about his legs aching. Dona said it was another attack of malaria, but he did not think so. They started to drive hard to get to Malamulo. It was a long, long way, and the roads were bad.

We stopped once in a while, and Dona cooked some food on the primus burner. She had brought some canned soups and some zwieback. We would eat, wash our dishes in some stream, and then be on our way again. Poor Bwana looked so pale that Dona was very worried. All she could think of was getting home with him so she could take care of him better.

He began to get such cramps in his legs that she stopped the car while he got out and walked them off. His face was drawn with pain. It was a real relief to get to Bulawayo, where the famous Solusi Mission is located, for the Seibenlists were there. Mrs. Seibenlist, a nurse, had Bwana take several grains of quinine and go to bed immediately. Bwana said he expected to get well right away if he took a good dose of quinine.

The next morning I asked Dona how he was.

"He is not a bit well," she said. "I was up and down with him all night. The quinine did not seem to have any effect."

The day was hot and humid, and it seemed as if disaster hung over us. Dona looked worried, and told me to pray for Bwana.

He was sick all that Sabbath day. He vomited up everything he ate or drank, even water. Pastor Seibenlist said that he thought we had better not try to go on toward Malamulo the next day, but Dona said, "He will want to go, for sick people like to be at home."

She was right. Bwana moaned when they suggested delaying the trip home. "I want to go home," he insisted. "I'd rather be there than anywhere else on the earth."

The next morning the Seibenlists again urged him to stay in bed, but he stubbornly dressed and declared he was ready to travel the 1,000 miles to Malamulo by way of Victoria Falls. He didn't look it. He stumbled and almost fell when he tried to walk, but walk he did, though he could not eat a bite of breakfast. He had not eaten for three days.

Bwana climbed boldly into the driver's seat to show the folks he was all right, and away we went. But before he had driven a mile from Solusi, in a pitiful voice he asked Dona to drive. She begged him to go back and rest a few days, but he refused. In my worry over Bwana, I scarcely thought of my own sadness at leaving Hulme back in Cape Town.

That day we traveled over terrible roads toward the line between Southern and Northern Rhodesia. The country was dry and rocky and wild, and there were few villages. The rainfall was so sparse that gardens could not grow, and of course people could not live without them.

Every little while Dona had to stop for Bwana to get out to vomit or walk on his tortured, cramping legs. He looked more sick every time we stopped, and I began to pray that God would not allow anything terrible to happen in my new family. I had seen death come swiftly so many times in Africa.

"I ought to have put my foot down and never come a step away from Solusi," Dona told me. "He is terribly sick. I don't know what we are going to do!"

By late afternoon we reached the customs gate between Northern and Southern Rhodesia. Bwana always took care of border crossings—papers, passports, luggage inspection—for he knew how his wife hated those details. He stumbled out of the car at the gates, swaying and weaving till I wondered if the officers would think he was drunk. He tried to fill out the papers, but it was too much for him. He had written only a few lines when he slumped over, and we had to help him into the car. Dona finished with the papers, and the men were a little easier on us than usual and let us through.

In this place we could hear a constant roar which was, they told us, made by the greatest waterfall in the world—Victoria. Dona drove to a camp near the falls, and rented a sort of hut for travelers. It had several soft beds in it and a cement floor. That was all. She got Bwana out, and while she made up the bed, I ran to get water. In a little while Dona had him in bed and had given him a cool sponge bath. He looked terrible.

I got the primus burner out, and Dona made a pot of potato soup. Bwana drank one cup of it, and quickly heaved it up. We did not feel like eating ourselves, he was so ill, and we were so afraid of what might happen. *Death comes so suddenly in Africa.*

Night fell, a wild, scary night that seemed alive with worries and terrors. Dona and I knelt by Bwana's bed and prayed.

Bwana went to sleep restlessly, breathing irregularly. A kind of cold sweat came out on his face. Dona kept a pan of water nearby and bathed his face and cracked lips every little bit.

"I don't see how I could face life without Bwana," she whispered to me, the tears starting from her eyes. "We have worked so hard together to build our lives so we could help do the work of God. We tried to raise our children right, so they would be a blessing to the world. Now, if this has to be the end—"

Somehow that night passed. Dona looked dead tired and white as marble. Bwana was much worse. He was hardly conscious, his eyes were half open, and his lips were almost black.

Dona came to my bed. "Get up, dear," she whispered. "It is daylight now, and you must run to the curator's house and ask him to come over. Unless we do something, Bwana cannot live. I know now that he has the blackwater fever."

I stared at her in horror. Blackwater fever! That is one of the most terrible diseases in the world. The mission cemetery is full of its victims. I stole a fearful glance toward poor Bwana, who looked more dead than alive. I do not think I ever dressed more quickly.

I was crying by the time I got to the curator's house, and the kind old man came right back with me.

He had a few words with Dona outside the door, as she whispered Bwana's symptoms to him. He said, "It is blackwater, all right, and your safest thing is to take him over to Livingstone. There is a hospital there with a good army doctor. He will save your husband if he can be saved."

With a stick he drew a little map on the ground by the door of the hut, so Dona would know how to get there. He and a native man and a tourist carried Bwana out to the car.

They left me at the hut, so I got busy and washed every dirty thing on the place, swept the yard, and cleaned the house. Then I lighted the kerosene iron and had the things all ironed by the time Dona returned. I could see she was still terribly worried, but she was a little relieved to know that something was being done for Bwana.

"The doctor said he is in a serious condition," she told me; "but when I left the hospital, the doctor and the nurses were working hard to save him." Dona went to the hospital again that afternoon, but she came back more discouraged than I had ever seen her.

"He is not so well. He could not eat a thing. I hope that when I go back in the morning he will be better. Surely after he has medicine all night he will be improved. Oh, Alice, I can't face life without him! He is the most precious person in my whole life!"

But the next morning he wasn't any better. Dona burst out crying so hard that I thought she was going to make herself sick. Then she told me what was the matter. She had passed a sawmill on her way to the hospital and began to think she would have to have those men make a box to put Bwana in, if he did not recover. She lay on the bed and cried and sobbed for a long time.

Early the next morning Dona started for the hospital, trying as she always did to be hopeful. "Surely he will be better today," she told me. "He has had time to take a turn for the better. I wish they'd let me stay there with him, but they won't. They say there is no place for me."

"I hope he is better; oh, I hope so," I said.

At twelve she was back. I knew by the way she ran that something was not right.

"He will die today! He will die today," she cried, "unless God will answer our prayers."

"Let's go out in the bush, Dona," I cried. *"Tikapemphere kupempherera Bwana Wokondewa!"* (Let us pray, let us pray, for dear Bwana.)

We started off on a walk across the bush to a place of privacy. Surely God would be gracious to us. Surely He would, for Bwana was so dear. He was *Wacifundo*, as the people called him—the merciful one. His tender, kindly ways had won everyone's hearts. Surely his good work was not done yet.

There was a giant baobab tree off there in the bush, with edible fruit on it. We knelt down there in the rough grass to ask God for the life of Bwana. I prayed first, and I suppose that everyone prays better in his mother tongue. I lapsed into the Xhosa, and with many tears begged God to spare the life that hung in the balance. Then Dona prayed.

When we got up, Dona looked at her watch. "It is just two o'clock," she said, worriedly. "The doctor said for me not to get too far away. I must get back."

# 18.

WHEN she came home that evening, Dona told me what had happened. She said when she got to the hospital she was almost afraid to go in. She crept in and peeped through the doorway. Bwana saw her.

"Come in, Mamma," he cried.

She was amazed, for he had been in a coma that morning. Now Bwana was smiling, and he told her it was at two o'clock when he felt a sudden change and sat up. When the attendants came in, his fever had left and his pulse and respiration had dropped to normal.

At two o'clock! Right when we were having prayer there by the big baobab tree!

I was almost speechless with joy, for I was one who had knelt and asked God to heal Bwana, and it was partly my prayer that was answered.

Later Bwana was released from the hospital, and we packed to resume our journey to Malamulo. Dona made him lie in the back seat so he could rest and regain his strength. Dona had two friends at Kalomo, about ninety miles from Livingstone. We had met them at Bulawayo, and they had urged us to stop sometime at their big cattle ranches and visit awhile.

We started from Livingstone about noon. It would give us the afternoon to get there, and we could rest at Kalomo and start early for Malamulo the next day.

The road was awful, and while Bwana was a great deal better, yet he was very weak. The doctor had warned Dona not to let him get cold or wet by any means. This could bring the fever back, and we might not win the next battle with death.

We did not get to Kalomo as quickly as Dona would have liked.

I saw that anxious look come into her face as she kept looking back at Bwana, who was sleeping lightly in spite of the rough road.

It was getting dusk, and worse than that, a chilly rain began to fall. Finally we drove into the tiny settlement which was Kalomo. There was a kind of hotel, though it did not look like one.

Dona got out in the drizzle and went into the hotel to inquire about the location of her friends' ranches.

Minutes later she came back with bad news: Both families were gone for the weekend, one to Bulawayo, and the other to Livingstone, from which we had just come. Furthermore, the hotel was full. Night was upon us, with cold, drenching rain.

Then the lady from the hotel came running out to the car. "Say," she said, "why don't you go to Namwianga Mission? It's out that road there not very far. Seven or eight miles, I'd say."

"Who runs it?" Dona asked her.

She flung out her arms. "I don't have any idea," she said, a little loftily. "They're all the same to me."

We turned the car and headed out the road the lady had indicated. Bwana still slept, with a wool blanket pulled over him. We crossed several "drifts"—places where a stream crosses the road. We would swoop down, splash through, and if lucky keep on going up the other side.

Ahead of us loomed a shape in the gathering twilight. "I think this is it," Dona said.

We saw no lights in the house. Suppose no one was at home? Dona drove to the side of the large dwelling and stopped.

Bwana awoke. "Where are we? Where are we?" he asked in a sleepy voice.

"Dona is finding out where to go," I said, hoping this was so.

In a minute she was back, smiling. "It's a Church of Christ mission," she said. "We are invited to stay in the guesthouse."

Someone with a bobbing lantern was opening a door in a thatched brick cottage near the main building. Dona drove near to the door, for it was raining quite hard by this time. She put a blanket over Bwana's head and whisked him into the house.

It was clean and inviting. A big bed covered with a mosquito-net canopy was turned down, and while I was bringing in the things we needed, Dona helped Bwana into bed. While we were getting our other possessions in, Mrs. Hobby's cookboy came in and filled a bowl with warm water. Bwana sighed with real comfort, all propped up with white, fluffy pillows. Dona was flying around, doing this and that, when the cookboy came in again, this time with a tray of food for Bwana. Dona and I were invited to the big house to eat with the Hobbys.

We took the umbrella and made a run for the house, where the Hobby family was waiting for us. It was fun to sit at the table in the lamplight, with Bwana alive, safe, and warm, and our world set at rights again.

After the meal I insisted on washing dishes, and told Mrs. Hobby to be sure to have Dona tell stories to her children.

Her face lighted up. "Oh, can Mrs. Edwards tell stories?" she asked me.

"Can she!" I cried. "You see the things, hear the things, and even smell the things when she tells stories. No one in the whole world can tell stories like Dona!"

Mrs. Hobby was obviously a good mother, and delighted in treats for her children. There were few enough treats in that isolated place. She had three boys, aged four to eight, and a tiny girl with hair the color of pinewood shavings and blue, blue eyes. She was so shy that she clung to her mother's skirt at a safe distance.

Soon Dona had those boys snuggled up by her knees, their eyes popping with excitement while she told them one story after another. The mother and father left to go to some kind of staff meeting. The shy little girl stayed near the kitchen door, but her big eyes never left Dona.

As I worked tidying the kitchen, I saw the little girl take tiny steps nearer and nearer till she was halfway across the room. Dona pretended she did not see her. The next thing I knew that child was standing beside Dona with her little elbows in the missionary lady's lap, looking up into her face. When I looked again, she was seated happily in Dona's lap.

When the Hobbys came home, they were amazed at the little girl. Mrs. Hobby said she had never made up to anyone.

We had a good night of rest and a fine breakfast. The Hobbys begged us to stay for the weekend, but Bwana was anxious to get to Malamulo. "They need us there," he told the Hobbys.

# 19.

As WE bade the Hobbys good-bye, they seemed like old friends instead of new ones. We got our car filled with petrol and headed eastward toward Nyasaland. The day was lovely, and we started out in high hopes.

We planned to sleep at a place near Beit Bridge, where the government had built rest houses for travelers. Then another day's journey, we thought, would take us to Mwami Mission, and one more day would easily get us home.

By hard driving we hoped to arrive at Beit Bridge by nine o'clock that night.

That evening, just after dark, Dona was driving as fast as she could on the bumpy road, when suddenly she put on the brakes and stopped. Bwana, who had been asleep, sat up. "What happened?" he asked.

"The rain has made this drift too dangerous to cross," Dona told him. "I think we had better sit here till morning."

"I don't want to sit here till morning," Bwana said, maybe a little impatient, for remember, he was sick and got tired easily. He was anxious to get to Beit Bridge.

With the lights shining on the water, Dona and I got out and waded across to see how deep it was. It was wider than a street, and the water came well above our knees. We came back.

"It isn't safe," Dona said. "The water will get in the engine and drown it out."

Bwana laughed good-naturedly. "I can take it across so fast the water won't have time to get into the motor," he said.

We got in. With a roar and a mighty splash, we got through the drift.

We no sooner reached the other side than I set up a cry. "My shoes! My red shoes!" Dona had her shoes on, but ah, me! I had forgotten and left mine sitting there on the bank. My pretty red shoes! Dona stopped the car and gave me the flashlight, and I waded back and got them.

When I got back, Dona tried to start the motor, but it was a dead bird. We could not move an inch. Not an inch. So there we sat. Dona and Bwana both groaned.

We were wretched. It was a clammy night, and this place had plenty of wild beasts. We could hear them crashing in the bush, and we could hear their cries. We had heard, too, that some of the native people nearby were hostile.

I was sure that night was going to last forever. I thought the sun was stuck some place over the eastern ridge. But when it did get unstuck, we saw we were in worse trouble. Then we found that all of our petrol was gone, every drop of it. The gas tank had hit a rock while we were splashing through the drift.

Morning came—a coldish, rain-spattery morning. We built a little fire. We made some powdered milk and ate it with bread. Then Dona and I set out to hunt a village. After a long walk we came to a place where we found a small school in session. We explained our plight, and the teacher let Dona send a boy for help. The nearest place, we learned, was an industrial school run by the Church of Scotland some thirty-five miles away. She told the boy that when he came back she would give him five shillings. His eyes sparkled at that. I could see he had never before owned five shillings all at once. He set out on a run.

We walked back to the car, prepared for a long wait. About two hours later a lorry came through on the way from Port Jameson to Lusaka. The driver promised to send back help from Lusaka.

We took everything out of the car and gave it a thorough cleaning. We went down to the drift and washed all our clothes and even took baths. We were safe. Few people came that way, and we were miles from any town.

Dona boiled potatoes and made soup for dinner. We ate picnic fashion by the side of the road. Bwana had blankets on the ground, where he slept and rested. We waited, straining our eyes and ears for some sound of approaching help. When the sun began to slant down toward the west, I saw the worried look return to Dona's eyes. Were we going to have to spend another horrible night cramped up in that car, surrounded by leopards, hyenas, and lions seeking food?

Suddenly we heard a motor throbbing in the stillness, and soon we saw a light shine out from across the drift. The water had gone down, and it was very shallow. Slowly the car came bumping across the uneven places. As Dona ran toward them, she began to cry as hard as she could cry. Two men got out of the car, patted her shoulders, and began talking to her.

"There, now, don't you cry, Mrs. Edwards. We came as soon as the boy got there. We'll help you."

Dona paid the little boy, who trotted off home as happy as a bee. He had five shillings, and the thrill of his first ride in a motor-car besides. He would be a king in his village for many days.

"Now, what can we do?" the Reverend Maxwell Robertson asked Dona.

"Take Mr. Edwards to your mission, and Alice and I will stay here," Dona said. "Someone may steal all we have if we leave things here."

In the end they did just that. Dona and I bedded down in the car, she in the back seat, I in the front.

We were almost asleep when someone knocked on the car window. It frightened us at first, but it was the kind lorry driver. He could get no help for us, and he had come all the way back to help us himself. When he saw we two were intending to spend the night there, he was horrified.

"You mustn't!" he said. "There is a very bad element of people through here. Some say there are cannibals or worse, and lions are so thick you'll be killed!"

When he could not persuade us to leave, he parked his car near ours and said he would stay in it to protect us.

We barely got settled down to sleep again when the sound of

another car broke the stillness. Traffic was heavy that night! This time it was a car from the Reverend Maxwell's Shalimbana Mission. It had come with a native watchman to care for the car, while we were instructed to go back to the mission with the driver. The mission folks had not aimed for us to stay there alone in the darkness.

Our kind truck driver went on back to Lusaka, since he saw we were safe. We were grateful to him, anyway. There were more good people in the world than I had dreamed possible. There were two kinds of white people—the very best and the very worst.

At the Shalimbana School, which we reached in the blackness of night, the ladies brought two tea trays, one for Dona and one for me. I never saw anything so inviting. We washed up, and did we eat! Every dish was cleaned out almost as if we had licked it. We did not lick them, of course. Dona would pulverize me if I did such an unmannerly thing as that! She always said she wanted me to be a lovely lady. But the steaming bowls of soup, the buttered bread, the cups of custard topped with guava jelly, and the pretty little frosted tea cakes disappeared swiftly.

Bwana lay there in bed smiling. "Isn't God good?" he kept saying. "The Lord has set us a table in the wilderness!"

That sounded so pretty to me. Dona told me it was a quotation from the Bible, and it means food appears where you least expect it.

# 20.

THE next day I got to help Mrs. Robertson prepare the food and wash the dishes. This lady was very kind. I told her lots of things about Malamulo, and of course Dona and Bwana ran through my stories like a bright stripe in a piece of cloth.

Later she and Dona sat and talked. It was sweet to see these two good people visiting together. They knew the same heart language.

On Easter Sunday, the following day, we made Bwana all comfortable and went to church, Dona and I. The Reverend Robertson was having the Communion for Easter service, and he invited Dona to the front with him. He served her first. Their service was a bit different from ours. In our church we use the unleavened bread broken up in small pieces to serve. Here they had pieces of yeast bread cut in small cubes.

The men at the mission pulled in our car, fixed the hole in the gas tank, and got it all ready for us. The Reverend Mr. Robertson would not let Bwana pay for the splendid, restful weekend. The care these fine people gave us was wonderful, and it made me more sure than ever of the watchcare of God that Dona had told me about so many times.

On Tuesday we started for Mwami Mission again. We passed that fateful drift, where we had broken our petrol tank and flooded our starter several days before. We inched across *carefully* this time, mindful of the sharp, ugly rocks lying in the shallow water. On the other side we saw evidences that elephants had been there that night, and the day before. They left great heaps of manure, and we saw that the tops were eaten off a number of small trees. We were surely glad we had been at the Shalimbana School when they went through. They are more dangerous than lions, and you are not even safe inside your car. Just let one of them come and sit on your car, and it's likely to crush your personality somewhat!

Nearly a week late we camped at the British rest camp near the Beit Bridge. A native caretaker had beds ready, so we ate and went to bed. The next morning Bwana said he would surely like to have some gravy and bread for breakfast. I built a fire, and Dona found a piece of old tin from somewhere. It was part of a broken car. We laid that on top of some stones, made a fire under the tin, and there was a stove good enough for anyone. We heated up two skillets. In one I fried some eggs while Dona made gravy in the other. We heated the primus burner to get hot water for rooibosch tea, the leaves of which grow down in the Cape. We laid slices of bread down on the tin by the side of the skillets, and there was as nice a toast as you would see anywhere.

Dona had a folding skillet with hinges in the middle. She made corn bread on an open fire several times in that thing, and once, for a fact, she made a cake. It was good, and we had some jam on it instead of the usual frosting. She made scones, too, fluffy and light. Bwana loved them.

It rained in the night there at Beit Bridge, and we heard wild animals snarling around down near the river. The wild animals come to drink when the darkness sets in. That is why it is dangerous to go to a river after sunset.

We drove across a mountain pass after that over a narrow, rough road with miles and miles of no-pass places. Bwana, since being sick, felt a little nervous, and kept calling out to Dona to be careful. He was a bad backseat driver for a while, when he suddenly realized what he was doing.

"Listen to me," he said. "I sound like some old woman!" He got his pillow then and took a nap, and we were glad.

We spent the weekend at Mwami Mission, where the mission director made us welcome. But we were anxious to get home. Sunday we got to Blantyre, and Monday to Malamulo and back to teaching again. It was my last year in secondary school.

# 21.

TWO years went by. I had not seen my lover for all those long, weary months. It seemed we would never get to set up the good home we had dreamed of and talked about. I began to doubt whether or not God was going to work out my bright dream. But Dona and Bwana never doubted.

In the meantime Dona let me use one of her big trunks for a "hope chest." Every girl who is going to get married ought to have one, so she said. No one at Malamulo had ever heard of such a thing. Every little while she would find something for me to put into it—a pretty dish, an embroidered tea towel, a bedspread she could spare. I got cloth when I could, and made pillowcases and dresser scarves. She drew patterns for me to embroider on everything. It was fun getting things ready for my very own home.

She told me that no one should enter into such an important phase of life as marriage without much thought and careful preparation. She told the other girls that, too. I had known of marriages at Malamulo where neither one of the couple owned even a cup or a spoon or a blanket. Dona said it was not sensible to start life like that. A person has more courage and self-respect if he has a few things for the home.

In time my hope chest was full of lovely things. Every few days students would come and want to see them.

One boy said, "I have decided that I will not marry until I have some things. This is the better way."

A girl said, "I am going to begin right now. Even if it has to be just one little thing a month, I will begin."

They would run to Dona to have her draw pictures on towels and pillowcases and little tablecloths.

Mr. Arnold Tyson-Flyn was head of the Malamulo Press. He

was a resourceful and ambitious man, and saw a more abundant and lucrative future for the Malamulo Press. Since the press needed an experienced man to run the new monotype machine and be assistant to Mr. Tyson-Flyn, the mission directors started to comb Africa for just the right man.

Would you believe it? The call went out for Mr. Hulme T. Siwundhla to take this excellent place. I was amazed, but Dona was not in the least surprised. "I knew the Lord would work it out," she said, as calmly as she would crack a peanut or peel a banana. "The Lord never fails us if we set our hearts to love and obey Him."

The day came at last when Hulme was to arrive at the Limbe train station from South Africa. That day seemed like a dream to me.

Dona and Bwana took me to the station to meet him. A thousand thoughts ran through my head. I was two years older than before. What if he didn't like me now? What if I didn't like him? "You will, silly," Dona laughed. "Every girl feels that way. And he will like you. How could he help it?"

"Did you get all outdone when Bwana came to see you?" I asked her curiously.

"Of course. Everyone gets panicky sometimes."

We stood off to one side when the funny little engine like a teakettle on black wheels, looking as important as a cockroach among ants, snorted into the station. I saw someone running along a coach, and he jumped right out of that train while it was still moving. It was Hulme! He looked even more handsome and wonderful than I had remembered.

We flew into each other's arms, and both of us began to cry, not minding a bit who saw us or heard us. Dona was mopping her eyes. So was Bwana.

"*Sithando Same,*" he called me in Xhosa—"Beloved!" It is *Okondedwa* in my language, but I knew just what he meant.

After he had kissed me ever so many times, he greeted Dona belatedly (she understood), and ran back to the train to get his things. Bwana drove the Jeep station wagon near the train so he could load his things in. He kept one arm around me all the time and helped load with the other. He said he wished I should *never* be out of his sight again.

Soon we were home, and we fixed Hulme up a room in a little guesthouse behind our house.

You never saw such a pair of mischief-makers as Dona and another missionary, Dona Ruth Phillips. One was bad enough, but the two of them! Did Hulme and I get teased all the time!

Dona heard that Hulme had been warned by everyone about lions, leopards, baboons, and snakes. He must have thought one would be behind every tree, for he was a little nervous at first when he walked to church or anywhere else after dark. I told him we were safe if we carried a light, but he had been filled so full of scary stories that he expected to meet a lion at every bend in the road. One night, just as Hulme told me good night and started to the guest cottage, Dona Edwards and Dona Phillips slipped into his bedroom ahead of him. We did not see them go, and I thought they were both in their bedrooms. Just as Hulme stepped into the little outer room he heard the most terrible growling and snarling and hissing from his bedroom.

You can imagine how he must have felt. And Dona can imitate animals so well that even the baboon himself would have been scared. Hulme backed out and ran to the Edwardses' house.

"Alice! Alice!" he called.

I met him at the kitchen door. "What's the matter, Hulme?" I asked.

"I forgot and left my door open," he said, his voice trembling. "Some wild beast has gotten into my room. I— I— can hear it. It's scratching terribly, and snarling. I don't know what to do. I don't dare to go in there."

"Come in a minute, Hulme. I want to go check on something. I'll be right back."

It came over me all of a sudden that it was just too quiet down the hall where Dona Phillips and Dona Edwards were supposed to be getting ready for bed.

I slipped down and knocked on Dona Phillips's door. No answer. Bwana Phillips was down the hill at a meeting with Bwana Edwards, and little Kenny Phillips was fast asleep. No Dona. Even her nightgown still hung on the door.

I slipped next door and opened the door ever so softly. The lamp was burning, the bed was turned down, but Dona Edwards was nowhere to be seen. I picked up Bwana's long flashlight, or "torch" as we call it, and went back to Hulme. I had to laugh.

"Don't worry about those 'wild beasts,'" I told him. "I can even tell you their first names. One is *Josephine* and the other is *Ruth*. It's another of their tricks. They invent more tricks than a witch doctor."

They screamed with laughter when I caught them hiding behind the bed, and we laughed too. Hulme said he was glad it happened, for it gave him a chance for another good-night kiss.

Arnold Tyson-Flyn (front, center), Malamulo Press manager, called Hulme (seated fourth from left) from Cape Town to join the printshop crew.  A. TYSON-FLYN

Alice Msumba and Hulme T. Siwundhla as an engaged couple.

Hulme and Alice on their wedding day with Pastor Edwards, who performed the ceremony.

# 22.

MY WEDDING dress lay in tissue paper in a long paper box, just as a friend of the Edwardses had sent it from America. Dona got me a lovely fingertip veil from Cape Town. My hope chest was crammed full of the prettiest things you could imagine. My three bridesmaids were fitted with pink crepe dresses. Dona Phillips was there all ready to help Dona Edwards with the wedding and to play the wedding march. (And, incidentally, also to help her play more tricks on Hulme and me.)

The day dawned clear and beautiful—my wedding day. It was Tuesday, June 17, 1952. Dona Phillips made me a heart-shaped bouquet on a frame she fashioned from a coat hanger. Mrs. Tyson-Flyn made a cake, a very tall one, with bride and groom on top. Dona made one like an open book with our names on it. How exciting!

For the feast, Dona invited all the teachers and their wives. She did not invite the children, for the crowd was almost a hundred as it was, and that is a lot of people to feed. Andy and Lester cooked all day. Such a feast! My mouth still waters to think of it! Dona made everything good she could think of, and she used her very best dishes.

I can still hear that wedding march played by the skillful fingers of Mrs. Ruth Phillips. The church was full. A pretty arch of flowers decorated the front. I came in with Camie, and there stood Hulme looking so handsome in his new black suit. He wore the nylon shirt Dona got him from America. He had to wear something from her.

Suddenly he and I stood there in front of dear Bwana Edwards, and the wedding ceremony began. Even though this was the most important moment of my whole life, I could hardly keep my mind

105

on the business in hand. Can't thoughts travel fast and jump around like the *kalulu* (rabbit)? I couldn't help thinking of that day when I cried in Dona's lap several hours, over a silly affair that had nothing to do with love. If it had not been for Dona I would never have known what I missed.

I didn't have long to meditate, as Bwana got to asking me some questions; and I knew I had better keep my mind on the ceremony or I might not say the right thing at the right time.

"Alice Princess Msumba, do you take this man, Hulme T. Siwundhla, to be your lawful wedded husband? Will you love him, honor him, and cherish him as long as you both shall live? Do you so promise?"

"I do!" I said, and I meant it with all my heart.

After we were prononuced husband and wife, Hulme gently put his arm around my shoulder, drew me to him, and kissed me in front of all those people. It surprised many of my African people, for I was the first African bride to be kissed in a church ceremony. Many times the Africans had seen missionaries kiss their wives, and had wondered what they were nibbling and gnawing on their wives for. The Cinyanja word for kissing is *kupysopysona*, which means to nibble and gnaw on something. So I was the first Nyasa girl to be "nibbled and gnawed on" at my wedding. It was wonderful, though. I was proud to be the first.

It is the African custom for a girl never to smile on her wedding day. If she does, she is considered a bad girl. But I could not help smiling constantly, for that's the way I felt. I had to break that custom. Dona always said bad customs were better broken than kept.

After our feast, served beautifully on the Edwardses' lawn, the Phillipses took us to Chileka where we spent our honeymoon at the quiet home of Pastor John Thomas. Then home—to the little guest house Dona let us have for our first home.

# 23.

WE HAD been married only two months when Bwana and Dona Edwards left Malamulo to go to America after seven years' hard work in Africa.

I could not bear for the day of their departure to dawn. I got up and stepped outside my door that last morning, and there she was on her veranda.

"Good morning, Peaches!" she called. She had called me Peaches ever since I lived with her.

I had to run inside and cry, and my husband tried to comfort me. Was this the last time she would say, "Good morning, Peaches"?

A little later I went to her house. "Don't go, Dona," I began, bursting out crying again. "Don't go. I can't bear it to have you go. I'll die if you do!"

"Neither of us is well, dear," she said. "Bwana's eyes haven't been right since he had that attack of blackwater fever, and we have not seen our Bob and Charlie for seven long years. We have three grandchildren we have never seen. We must go, darling. Bwana needs to get better."

I could see it was selfish for me to want them to stay in that disease-laden country, when with my own eyes I had seen Bwana so terribly sick. Yet how could I live without a mother and a father? I stood in the depot in Limbe the day they left and cried myself sick. They wept, too.

"Listen, Alice," Dona said. "I am going to see what I can do about helping you and Hulme come to America for a college education. I do not know if I can do it, but I can if it is the will of the Lord. You just pray hard that God will help me to know His will for you. I want to see you get a real preparation for your lifework, and I know you cannot get it here. I firmly believe we will be together again in America."

You can't know how precious this faint glimmer of hope was to my heart. I knew Dona's iron determination so well; I knew if she made up her mind to do a thing, she would do it if she had to move a mountain a rock at a time. If anyone could get us to America and to college, Dona could.

The Tyson-Flyns took us to Limbe to see them off. Many of the students had come, too, and some were mourning and crying. It was a heartbreaking scene. One poor old woman brought Dona a dozen eggs to help her with her food on her journey.

When I saw that train pull out, taking Dona and Bwana, the beat of those iron wheels seemed to grind the very heart out of me. I screamed, and Hulme had to hold me or I would have run down the tracks after the train. Dona and Bwana leaned far out of the window watching us, tears streaming from their eyes. I cried till I could hardly see my way to the car. Mr. Tyson-Flyn was very kind to us. My new husband was very tender. I could hardly bear to go back to the place so filled with memories. Life would never be the same again.

The house looked so empty and sad, as if it had lost its soul. The piano was sold, the red rug gone. Someone had bought the big refrigerator. Dona's vases, doilies, pretty dishes, and knick-knacks were all packed. Everywhere I saw reminders of gay times, jokes, tricks, and laughter. Dona loved to play tricks to keep folks happy and in good humor.

Andy Sandula, the cook boy, came out on the back porch with his things tied in a little bundle to go to his home. I saw tears on his dark cheeks. He shook his head as he went away, unable to speak.

We all wept that evening—Camie, Hulme, and I. We could hardly eat. Then we took heart and wrote some letters. We addressed them to the *Llangibby Castle,* whose first stop would be the Island of Zanzibar. Our letters would await them there. Talking to my precious ones even on paper was a little comfort.

# 24.

ALMOST everything I had, I owed to the Edwardses. Little by little they had supplied the furniture for our house. Dona gave me a dresser, and I had a bed with a good innerspring mattress. When Mrs. Pierce got her new divan set, Dona and Bwana bought the old one for me. They gave us the money to have a floor put into our house and to put matting on the ceilings. My dishes all came from them, also my rugs. Mrs. Kotz let me have a nice round dining table and I had a neat dish cupboard. Our house was on Line One, as they call the row of houses where the African teachers and ministers live.

Everywhere I looked were mementos of dear Mother and Father. I had a special drawer for their letters. I read these until they were breaking in two at the folds.

I did not see how the Edwardses could possibly get us to America, especially now since I was married to my Hulme. But they loved Hulme, too, and liked that complication.

One day amazing news came, though nothing should have amazed me after all that had happened already. They had gotten to their son Bwana Bob's in Los Angeles, California, after long weeks of travel, and Dona had not been there an hour before a friend gave her a hundred dollars for "any project she might be interested in, in Africa."

"As if I don't have a project that I'm interested in!" Dona wrote.

She said she had wondered if it was God's will for her to bring Hulme and me to America. So many people told her, "If you take them to the States you will 'spoil' them." I got so I hated that word "spoil" worse than swear words. I've seen spoiled people, and they weren't always Africans either! Did Dona spoil me? You should have seen her make me toe the mark. My! I would rather she had beaten me than to scold me and talk to me the way she often did. Those lectures in the living room, with Dona's pointing finger emphasizing every sentence, made me decide to quit doing the wrong thing.

Every letter I got, Dona had more money. Three hundred dollars. Five hundred. People were calling her to talk about Africa. Everywhere she went someone gave her money for us to come to America. After lecturing in one city she received $900. Now we were sure of going to America, with Dona raising money so fast, like a leopard running. Nothing would stop her. Once Bwana had said, with a hearty laugh, "There are three things that won't wait for anyone: time, tide, and my wife."

One *akuru-akuru* (Cinyanja for V.I.P.) said, "Your Dona just doesn't know the situation. She means well, but you'll never get your passport, and that's all there is to it. She shouldn't get you all stirred up about it and then let you down in disappointment."

Others felt duty bound to offer what they called "good, solid advice." "You don't want to go to America," was the way they usually started. That sentence irritated me almost beyond endurance. How, in all wisdom, could they know what I wanted?

Then one day I realized I was going to have a baby. While teaching, I began to feel nauseated, and soon I could hardly stand the sight or smell of food. The fumes from our little stove made me so sick that I had to run out of the house and walk around until Hulme was through cooking.

Then, as I would lie down in our hot little bedroom, I would think of Dona's bottles of cool mulberry juice and grenadilla juice from the refrigerator. Oh, for something cold!

I hated to tell Dona about the baby, because that would complicate things for her, and they were already complicated enough. I knew, too, that those who liked to give us advice would be saying, "Now you can't go, of course. With a baby to care for, you *can't* go to school. You might as well decide to stay right here. You don't want to go to America, anyway."

*"You don't want to go!"* That phrase alone was maddening. I did want to go worse than I wanted anything.

Sometimes we got boxes while we waited for Dona to raise that great sum of money. Once, a bright aqua skirt came for me and a frilly pink nylon blouse. I had never owned one like it before.

When I unfolded the skirt, I realized then that Dona had really bought that skirt for herself. When she made up my box she had just pulled it out of her closet and packed it, not thinking of her sweet, dear self and her needs at all! She was always doing things like that!

In the pocket I found her hanky, crumpled up by pressure from her hand. It touched my heart so, that for weeks I could not bear to wash it and iron out those creases. Someway, Dona's hanky, lying on my dresser just as she had touched it, brought her nearer to me.

We lived for news from America. In a typical letter, she would say, "I went to Shafter, California, today. They gave me $160 for your fund." All Americans must be good or they would not put money out like that. She told of a colored woman who gave her vacation money for us. She donated £15-0-0 in our money. I worked three months for that much salary. It was unbelievable. What kind of place *was* America, anyway, of which we were hearing so much?

Meanwhile, I made little clothes for my babe. As nearly as I could figure, he or she would be born in April sometime, when the heavy rains were abating and cooler weather was beginning. We had a month's vacation coming in April, and that would help me get used to caring for a child. Later I could make arrangements for a student to care for him while I was in school.

People took a kind interest in us. Mrs. Tyson-Flyn gave me things her baby had outgrown, and we bought a baby bed from her, too. This bed—screening covered all sides—was just the thing for Africa. No deadly mosquitoes must bite my baby!

Dangerous ants called *lintumbu* infested the area, too. These have been known to eat whole pieces out of little babies' heads and helpless invalids at night. They will kill all the chickens in a hen-roost, till nothing is left but bones and feathers. Down by the hospital I once saw a snake covered with these horrible ants. If they attack you, you don't always know it until about a million bite you at once all over your whole body. I did not want these dreadful things to hurt my little one, so we prepared ahead for its safety.

A. TYSON-FLYN

Malamulo Hospital, where Lowell and Thelma Siwundhla were born.

# 25.

I HAD no idea there were such pains in this wide world. If a big leopard could reach in and tear and claw at my middle, it could hurt no worse. I was seized with these pains one April night, and Hulme and I walked together the quarter of a mile to the maternity ward. I had to stop every little bit and bend double with pain, and once I looked up at the night sky set with bright stars; then I looked off to the northwest. Far away, around the curve of the earth, was Mother, dear Dona Edwards, and how I needed her now! If I could just tell her how painful this thing was and hear her voice telling me I would be all right, it would be a lot easier.

Then we were at the hospital, where Miss Mary Ford, the head nurse, took me in hand. I felt better knowing such a capable person was in charge.

The doctor gave me something that helped a little, but not much. Then I heard the nurse say, "It's a little boy." Then they gave me some medicine and I went to sleep. When I woke up, Hulme was sitting by my bed grinning. He had a son!

Anyway, I was delighted. A little boy—Hulme's and mine! Oh! If Dona and Bwana could only see him! They would be crazy about him, too.

Hulme set up some elaborate birth announcements at the mission press. Soon news of Lowell Hulme Thembalihle Siwundhla took flight across the sea. It had to be Lowell, of course; that was Bwana Edwards's name.

I wondered often what I had done with my time before that baby came. Quiet afternoon hours I had formerly spent were gone forever. Now Lowell's little pants had to be washed, and his little body kept clean and sweet. "Nobody likes a dirty baby," Dona had often said to me.

When Baby Lowell was two and a half years old, I realized I was pregnant again. Now the personal visits began again, as our well-meaning friends dolefully predicted we would never go to America. I believed them myself this time. Not one child, but two. What would Dona say?

"We will make it," she wrote, when she heard the news. "We have almost enough money. Why don't you apply for passports?"

We decided to spend our vacation at Solusi Missionary College, near Bulawayo, Southern Rhodesia. Our main idea was to see the American consul about our passports. Meanwhile people kept telling us we ought not to go to America. We had plenty of fine advice all the time, all unsolicited, all free.

"Your work is here," they would say. "You'll not want to come back if you go to America." "The people here won't like your going away and won't accept you again." "You'll never be the same if you go away."

But we kept on hoping and praying we could go to America. I knew we would, in spite of everything. Dona and Bwana had prayed and had gotten the "go-ahead" from God. The years I lived in the big brick mission house with them had given me an unshakable faith in the impossible—at least if that extraordinary couple were working on it.

# 26.

WE TALKED with Dr. Clark, who was president of Solusi College. He gave us every encouragement to attend school there. But deep in our hearts we still hoped to go to fabulous America.

America seemed a place like the seven golden cities of Cibola that Coronado tried so hard to find. People tried to find them all through the years, but never did. Would we find America? Some way we knew by the set of Dona's chin that we would. So we committed ourselves only vaguely to Dr. Clark's kind invitation.

We stopped off at the city of Salisbury to visit the American consul. In the tall building to which we were directed, Hulme consulted the bulletin board learnedly. I watched him curiously, for I had lived in the bush so many years that tall buildings, elevators, and escalators were things I'd heard of but experienced only briefly while Dona and Bwana were on furlough.

Then Hulme learnedly punched a button. We entered the elevator, ascended to the proper floor, and got off. His worldly wisdom filled me with awe.

The plate-glass sign in front of the offices looked impressive. We stood and read it before we timidly opened the door to enter the reception room. Would someone shout at us and tell us to wait outside in the hall? Would we be yelled at if we dared sit down in a chair in the lovely reception room? We were both so tired. The baby was heavily asleep in Hulme's arms, and my legs felt like boiled macaroni.

You have to have a dark skin to realize the fears and timidity we always felt. But America began to look lovely and different to us as the consul, great man that he was, greeted us kindly, warmly, cordially. He treated us like *people*. Our fears vanished as he made us sit down in big, comfortable upholstered chairs.

He pulled up his chair, ruffled through papers, and listened most attentively to our plaintive little tale. He remembered having had correspondence with our Pastor W. D. Pierce of Blantyre on this same matter. He took out the folder and reviewed the case thoroughly with our help.

The consul gave us cold water from his own cold-water fountain. Then he told us to wait awhile, for he was going down to see the South African consul.

After he had breezed out of the door, Hulme and I looked at each other in amazement.

"He's *interested* in us!" he exclaimed, incredulously.

"He is!" was all I could answer.

Little Lowell went to sleep, and we laid him on the big divan. In a few minutes the consul returned with a sheaf of papers in his hand, exuding confidence and friendliness.

"Now look, Mr. Siwundhla," he said, "you take these forms home with you to Nyasaland. Fill them out carefully, and return them *to me. I* will be the one to take them to the South African consul. I have told him about you, and when I give him the papers, I can refresh his memory. We consuls have so much to do, we sometimes forget that behind each request is a person to whom it is vitally important."

He assured us he would do all he could do to help us. Such politeness; such deference. Why? Because he was an American, like Dona and Bwana!

Our hearts were light as we took our journey on the rickety train back to Malamulo, Nyasaland, and our small home on Line One.

# 27.

IT TOOK a lot of doing to make all the preparations. Dona and Bwana were to assume the responsibility of our being in America. A school on the approved list—in our case, Oakwood College, Huntsville, Alabama—was to accept us. The Edwardses had picked out this college for us to attend, and we knew we would like it or they would not have picked it.

Hulme is an orderly soul; and he loves detail work, which I hate. So he took charge of the paper work.

The Edwardses sent us the $300 we needed, and finally we sent the big envelope to the American consul in Salisbury.

Time dragged. You have to wait a long time to get official things done. At last, to our joy and surprise, an official envelope came which actually contained the Union of South Africa passport for my husband. This is what people said was impossible to get.

We shouted for joy. We ran next door and showed it to our neighbors, the Samuels, who had never laid eyes on a South African passport before.

My husband showed it to the workers at the mission press, whose eyes bugged out. We dressed up and took the miraculous booklet to the Pearsons. They had doubted we would ever get it, though they were hoping something might work out for us.

We took it everywhere, until by nightfall everyone knew Hulme Siwundhla actually had his passport to go to America. Later we learned that the same day his had been issued, the government had turned down more than 800 other applications.

I still had my passport to secure. I was a British subject, a citizen of Nyasaland, and no one thought I would have any difficulty.

We got the forms to fill out in Blantyre, and started to fill them out. Then we came to the part about a birth certificate. Of course I did not have one, for people were not so careful to record native births when I was a child. Besides, many babies were born just anywhere: on the path to the village, in the garden, by the waterside, or in the kitchen hut. I took my forms to Pastor Rex Pearson, our mission director, to see what advice he would give. Now that Hulme had his passport, I *must* get mine.

My baby girl needed me, as well as my boy. The girl was not easy to care for either. She was demanding, and at times sickly and fretful. But I had to leave her with bottles and formula (which Africans don't approve), and go forty miles to Cholo to find a magistrate. That took all day. But my husband was waiting for me at the bus stop at Malamulo; he never failed me. At least I had secured my affidavit; I looked forward to a day at home.

But my husband said, "Now, tomorrow, honey, you must take this to Blantyre to the immigration office."

I almost burst into tears. I had had such bright dreams of being at home, dusting and polishing and sweeping, and washing out little garments. I'd thought of the precious feel of my baby in my arms in the cool of the evening, and of little Lowell building his endless tunnels in the sandpile.

How could I face another hot day on the bumpy bus smelling of vomit, unwashed bodies, and moldy food? But Hulme was wiser and stronger than I, and his good judgment prevailed.

After the three-and-one-half-hour trip, I took that precious affidavit to the immigration office.

"You will have to get a letter from your chief," the man told me, "to prove your father's citizenship. You'll have to have a marriage certificate, a letter of acceptance from the college, a letter from your sponsor showing full responsibility while you are in the United States. This must be signed before an attorney." I also had to have a deposit of £150 to guarantee my return to Africa. The red tape bewildered me.

After we rounded up those things, we sent them to Zomba, the capital. Then we waited and waited and waited, till I was so tense I wanted to scream.

But not Hulme, the dear, methodical soul. When we got tired enough of waiting, he just got on the bus and went to see what was happening. Hulme is so persevering that at last they gave him my passport.

I met him at the bus when he returned. As soon as he got off the bus, I saw joy shining through the lines of weariness and tension. He took the handles of the baby's pram, and handed me a book, a black book, three inches by six, with my name on it!

My passport! I couldn't believe it! Acting like my sister Tillie, I ran to and fro on the road squealing and screaming out. I could not help it. I had to tell everyone. Here they were, both of them. *Two* mountains moved!

We stopped at the mission director's house in our glee. Pastor Rex Pearson's face wore first a look of unbelief, which changed to one of delighted surprise. He invited us into his living room. Seizing my hand, he said, "Alice, if you get spoiled, it won't be because you went to America. You're spoiled already."

We walked back rejoicing to our little brick house. But Hulme, in his quiet, methodical way, knew we were not through yet. There were visas to get in order to enter the United States. Again people told us we would never get these permits. They even hinted that visas were harder to get than passports. How could that be true?

So Hulme went to Salisbury to see the good American consul again. This man had moved mountains for us, and we had faith he could and would move a few more.

Again the consul was more than kind. Not only did he give Hulme the forms to fill out, but he made personal contacts with doctors to examine him for a long list of diseases. The consul also gave him directions as to what I should do to get my visa. When my husband came home Friday he was sick with malaria, but he saw to it that I filled out my forms promptly. I flew to getting the needed things for my visa. I was examined, X-rayed, tapped, picked, and scrutinized for more diseases than I knew existed.

We wrote Dona and Bwana exuberantly. We had climbed

mountains of difficulties, and readied ourselves for our booking. That looked easy, because we had heard that ships sailed to and fro on the ocean all the time—thousands and thousands of them. But here we ran into a difficulty we had not dreamed of. No one could get us a booking to America on anything. A war was going on in the Suez, and that tied up all shipping, it seemed. We could not dream of airplanes because we knew Dona and Bwana did not have that kind of money. It cost thousands of dollars to go flying up among the clouds. Airplanes frightened us anyway.

For the first time I saw Hulme almost discouraged. Here was something he could not change. The war had spoiled our dreams.

"We'll wait now on the Lord," Hulme said at last. "If He has brought us thus far, He knows a thousand ways of helping us that we know nothing about."

Friday afternoon we scurried like mad to our home to get ready for the Sabbath. The house looked lovely when we polished the red cement floors with *"stoep* polish" and the scarves and clothes and linens were bright and clean.

I worked in the kitchen, stirring up a guava-sauce cake that Dona had taught me to make. Bwana had liked applesauce cake so well in the States, that Dona took the same recipe and substituted guava sauce. Delightful!

# 28.

LATER that afternoon we had our house spotless. Our Sabbath clothes, clean and pressed, we laid out just as I had been taught. Hulme busily cleaned our shoes behind the house.

Suddenly his keen brown eyes spotted something unusual. He saw a car head down the grassy, mud-rutted hill toward our house. I had the cake almost ready for the oven.

"Alice, someone is coming," he called. "You go meet them—I've got polish all over my hands!"

"I can't," I protested. "The cake is ready to go into the oven. You go."

"Honey, it's Pastor and Mrs. Pierce, and Pastor Pearson, and Mrs. A. V. Edwards. They've stopped, you've *got* to go meet them!"

"My cake!" I cried.

"My dirty hands!" he cried.

It ended up that we both went, for all of a sudden a terrible fear came over me that someone had died. Otherwise, why should so many people come? We moved mechanically to the door.

"Who is dead?" I cried.

"No one is dead, Alice," Bwana Pierce said, his face wreathed in smiles. They all got out of the car, and Dona Pierce followed her husband up the walk. There was a smile on Myrtle Pierce's face, too. The director of the mission and Mrs. A. V. Edwards followed.

"We have good news for you. May we come in?" Pastor Pierce opened our screen, and they all walked in. They filled up our davenport and chairs, and Hulme and I stood there waiting, too excited to sit down. Who cared about the guava cake and the shoes?

"Are you ready for the good news?" Bwana Pierce asked.

"Yes," said Hulme quietly, "let us hear it."

"Could you be ready to leave for America right away?" he asked. We gasped.

"Are you joking?" I asked.

"No, I'm not joking you. I got a phone call this afternoon all the way from America. They said to get you ready to come immediately by *ndege* [airplane]."

"*Ndege!*" Hulme and I cried in unison. "*Ndege?*"

This so amazed us that we all knelt down to pray by common consent. We said that whichever way we felt after praying, that would be the way it would be.

After we got up from our knees, we told them that if God willed for us to go to America, we would go.

Then Mr. Pierce went into detail. He said he was walking into his office as usual when the phone rang. To his amazement, it was America calling, asking him* to invite Alice and Hulme Siwundhla to come to America immediately by airplane.

"Since when have Bwana and Dona become so rich as to send us by *ndege* to America?" we asked. "To go by *ndege* would cost thousands of pounds."

He paid no attention to my protests. "To travel by *ndege*," he continued, "you cannot take very much *katundu* [luggage]. You can take only bare necessities, and the Edwardses will give you what you need in America."

He said he had to return to Blantyre and call up America and give an answer. And he explained that the Edwardses had no great stack of money, so far as he knew, but Mrs. Edwards was a great one for finding friends, and she had found someone to finance this *ndege* trip.

Our minds whirled. He kept on talking and smiling, and smiling and talking.

"This is the first time America has ever called by phone to Central Africa or Nyasaland," he said, obviously thrilled. "It stirred up the whole town. Right there in my little office I was talking to a man on the other side of the world! To a man in Hollywood, California!"

I knew my geography, and I couldn't help exclaiming at that.
"Los Angeles?" I cried. "Dona and Bwana live in New York!"
"They have friends *everywhere*," he reminded me, "and this
particular friend lives in Los Angeles. He has lots of money. That
telephone call alone cost fifteen dollars a minute, and we talked for
fifteen minutes!"

Soon they were gone and Hulme and I were left staring at each
other across our little sitting room. My guava cake had bubbled
up and spoiled. The shoes remained half polished. But our little
boy had escaped, and I could hear his treble voice over on the
porch of the Samuels, who lived next door. Before we could speak
to each other, our neighbors the Samuels—Fales and Master—
burst in upon us.

"What is this your child is saying?" asked Master, his eyes
glowing.

"It can't be true," my husband answered.

"No, it can't," I echoed. "We have dreamed too long. It can't
be real!"

"Now listen!" Fales seized me and shook me. "Is it true what
little Lowell says? He says you are going to America. When?"

It jarred me to my senses a little bit. I looked at her a little
foolishly, hardly realizing what she was saying.

"We're to go right away," Hulme answered. "On the *ndege*—
the airplane. Dona and Bwana have friends who are rich."

"But when?" queried Master.

"Bwana Pierce has gone into town to call up America on the
telephone. Now, they are telling them that we will go."

A smile broke over Hulme's face. "Of course we must go. It
is God who has opened the gates and will carry us through the air
to the college. It is a miracle."

I tried to bake my bubbled-up guava cake; but it was a failure—
and who cared? There were too many wonderful things to talk
about, and my mind danced to a kind of rhythm: "I'll soon see
Bwana with his kind, loving face. I'll soon see Dona, who is so
funny and unpredictable."

Problems buzzed around my head like gnats from the bush, but I decided to make them wait while I thought about seeing Dona and Bwana and the exciting trip on the *ndege,* which I never saw except high in the air.

That night I lay in bed stiff as a piece of *mlombwa* wood in the carpenter shop. I thought I must not move or I'd wake Hulme, which would not be fair. He was still, too. Finally I could stand it no longer.

"Hulme," I whispered softly.

"Huh?" he answered quickly. I knew he had been lying there like *matabwa* (lumber) himself.

"I can't sleep or relax or do anything."

"Neither can I."

We finally decided to get up and slip off to the hospital to see if they could help us.

We looked at the children, but they were sleeping as usual. Through the darkness we made our way to the hospital.

They were sympathetic, for our exciting news had flown everywhere. They gave us some tiny pills to take when we got home.

We took them, but they had no effect on us. We continued to lie awake, excited and trembling, until morning.

They told us we could take only the most necessary articles on the airplane. Diapers, of course, and a few changes of clothing for Lowell and the baby.

We had a hard time picking and choosing, for we had worked hard for years, and pinched pennies and hunted bargains, for the things we owned. We had pretty things that Dona and Bwana had given us, too, and we dreaded to just close the door and leave them all. But the Pierces and the Pearsons said they would help us pack and store these treasures away, especially what we did not want to sell. There were plates and dishes made precious by the memory of our dear ones eating from them, and furniture Bwana's handy hands had fixed. Now we were about to walk out and leave them all.

My eyes swept our little home. Dona and Bwana had given us

money to cement the floors, make window and door screens, and install ceilings out of clean matting. Our house was easier to care for and healthier to live in than any other in Line One.

As the time drew near to leave, we felt vaguely fearful of the unknown ahead of us. But at the end of the *ndege* flight dear Bwana and Dona, who loved us as their own children, waited for our coming. This thought buoyed us up.

A. TYSON-FLYN

Domestic building, or girls' school, where Alice attended classes and later served as a teacher.

# 29.

THE word got all over the mission that we were to go by *ndege* to America, to college, and to Bwana and Dona.

Pastor and Mrs. Pierce took us to the Chileka Airport out of Blantyre, more than forty miles away. The Pearsons and Mrs. Bristow followed along after us. My, but it was exciting to be the center of attraction. Little old me, whom Dona and Bwana found so needy and so ragged. The news had leaked out in Blantyre and Limbe, too, and in all the villages around, that an *African family* was actually going up in one of those big metal birds. As we approached the plane at the airport, we saw Likagwa, a teller at the Barclays Bank. How did everyone find out so fast about our journey?

Soon the big *ndege,* with us Africans inside it, took off and whisked us to Salisbury, Southern Rhodesia, in a mere hour or so. Here we were to see the American consul.

But at Salisbury we met disappointment. To our chagrin, we learned that Hulme's passport had not been endorsed for the countries through which we would have to pass. The *ndege* flew away without us, and we had to wait several days for an answer to a barrage of telegrams which the good American consul sent to Pretoria. The officials in South Africa apparently ignored them.

The waiting was not as easy as it sounds. No hotel would allow us to stay all night, nor would the restaurants serve us food. If you think Africa was *our* homeland, you should have walked in some African's shoes—if he had any. There we were with two tiny children, and if it had not been for a Mr. Pangani, we would have had no place to sleep at night. *The African Daily News* headlined a front-page story, "Nyasa Family on Way to U.S.A. Stranded in Salisbury."

Mr. Pangani, who worked in the India House, heard of our difficulty and opened his home to us.

Finally the consul said he was going to put us on a nonstop flight to London, and we would not need any of those old endorsements. His telegrams had not been so much as acknowledged.

However, by this time the American ambassador in South Africa had visited the Minister of the Interior in Pretoria, and had secured permits to travel through Nairobi, Khartoum, Rome, Italy, London, Copenhagen, and across the North Pole to Los Angeles.

At last we boarded the big airliner with a hundred other people. In a few minutes we were flying high in the air, as lovely Lake Nyasa sparkled below us.

How beautiful that big B.O.A.C. looked! Pretty blue seats with white covers for passengers' heads. Stewards and stewardesses also dressed in becoming blue and white.

I just sat there thinking of Dona Edwards, the only mother I had. She would likely say "Hello, Peaches," as she used to do, when we arrived.

Little Lowell sang little songs of his own composing about Gogo Lowell and Gogo Josalina (Josephine), but they were all mixed up with "Cholo Mountain far, far away." The little soul had no idea of distance, nor had I. Meanwhile our airplane zoomed through the sky over Kenya, Uganda, Ethiopia, and Somaliland. Eventually it came down on the hot runway in Khartoum, far up on the map of Africa, south of Egypt.

We got out, and bought Dona a little pocketbook and an inlaid box, souvenirs of that strange place. Men stood about in long gowns with side sashes, their horny feet thrust into rough sandals. They wore turbans wound about their heads, and their black eyes gazed at us solemnly.

There was a sameness, it seemed to me, to their countenances. They had thin noses and lips, white teeth, and deep-set black eyes. "Moslems, I am sure," I told myself.

Someone told us that winter was beginning in America. When we left Nyasaland it was summer, but now we had crossed the equator into the northern hemisphere. Here was I, all dressed in summer clothes with a white straw summer hat, and even white gloves.

That evening the slim, pretty stewardess stood up and made her announcements. She told us her name, and said if we needed anything, just to ask for it. Then she said they would serve us a cocktail dinner that night.

The British had told us that the word for the *tambala*, or rooster, as Americans call it, is "cock." I was greatly puzzled at her remark; a meal made from the cock tails did not sound particularly appetizing, especially since I was beginning to get a little airsick. A passenger told me "cocktail dinner" simply meant a "very good dinner."

In our years at the mission we had never eaten the black fish, the snake, the rat, or certain other creatures, as do many of the heathen. So when the courses began to arrive, we didn't know what to do.

First, there were sea creatures like crayfish. We could see their veins and claws, and they were sitting up on the plate looking at us. I seized the little sack and was sick. The astonished stewardess removed our plates, but came back confidently smiling. Surely, she thought, we would eat the ham, but we didn't. When neither of us could eat, they brought us liquor, which we could not drink. I know we were problem children, for everyone else was eating with gusto. They liked the cocktail dinner.

Rome came into view. As we looked down on the ancient city clustered about the seven hills, we thought of Bwana's history classes and how real he made the history of the world. Here was the home of the Roman Catholic Church and of the pope.

Before long we were on our way again, flying high over the snowcapped Alps, across France to London. We got there at 3 o'clock in the morning, tired but filled with wonder. Was it only yesterday we climbed on the plane? The bed was soft and clean at the Stanley Arms Hotel. We went to sleep right away. Late in the morning, a tea wagon full of good, appetizing food was trundled *into* our room. Toasted English muffins, eggs, milk, jelly, porridge, and even bottles for little Thelma. It was a welcome sight after that "cocktail dinner."

We wanted to see London, and when we expressed our desire, here came a taxi to take us for a "tour." We protested that we had no money, but the hotel folks told us that "the folks in America are taking care of this." Had Bwana and Dona found a gold mine?

We saw the beautiful Buckingham Palace where our good Queen Elizabeth resides. Then we saw Westminster Abbey where the great missionary David Livingstone lies sleeping. Very few Africans have not heard of him and his wonderful work of stopping the slave traffic in central Africa.

London! We had heard of that city all our lives, and here we were right in the heart of it. Still, it was wonderful to stretch out on a bed, even though we were mixed up about day and night.

I bathed the baby and little Lowell in the gleaming white English bathroom, so different from our crude accommodations back at Malamulo. Again they brought in food in a kind of tea wagon. Then, after we ate, we bathed and fell into the clean beds.

It seemed we had hardly fallen asleep when the phone rang. I did not understand what the English operator said, so I kept repeating, "Pardon. Pardon." Then someone knocked at our door. "You are to get ready to go by plane to New York," a man told us. "The taxi will be here in a few minutes."

Still sleepy, we dressed, and were soon riding through a thick fog on our way to the great London Airport. I can dimly remember being hustled through to a great plane. I walked like one in a dream. Little Lowell whimpered and stumbled. They settled us, and we automatically fastened our seat belts as the signals directed.

On this plane a stewardess also stood up and made her announcements. She told us how high we would fly, and what kind of weather we would have. She said we would reach New York in twelve hours.

Then she got out an orange-colored thing that looked like a hot-water bottle. She told us to look under our seats and we would each find one. We looked, and we did. She blew this strange thing up and put it on herself like a jacket. She said that up to now we had been flying over land, but now we would cross the mighty Atlantic. (What a thrill! We had read about the Atlantic Ocean in our African geographies.)

She said that in case our plane went down at sea, we should put on the life preservers. Then we were to push the doors marked EXIT, and jump out, and float. Oh! That scared us! When we asked about life preservers for our children, she said we would just have to hang on to the children!

All things terrifying come to an end sometime. The big bird drew nearer to land, and we could see the thicket of spires and towers of Manhattan far below. The seat-belt light flashed, and my heart filled with joy. In a few moments we'd see Bwana's patient, kind face and Dona's sparkly one, full of fun and mischief. We'd hear Bwana's booming laugh. He laughed as no one else we ever heard, clear down to his heels. We would smell delightful odors from Dona's kitchen and see the table set with the lace tablecloth Auntie Edna Van Wagner crocheted for her. There would be candles lit in the Indian brass candlesticks Bwana got for her birthday. She would use her beautiful blue Portuguese china; she'd—

But here! We had landed, and no Dona and Bwana stood at the fence waving and beckoning. We waited for the American citizens to leave first. Then we had to show the Health Department the certificates they required. They went through all our things, even the bag of our baby's wet diapers. Then, after a tedious wait, we were told to go back to the gates again and board an American Airlines plane, Flight 671, for Los Angeles!

"We don't want to go to Los Angeles," I cried. "Our sponsors live right here in New York! Los Angeles is too far away. I have seen it on maps. They will wonder what became of us. We'll be lost in this strange land and have no money, no blankets!"

Tears were springing in my eyes. Had God and Dona and Bwana forsaken us? What would become of us?

It was strange, but the airplane people all seemed to know about our case. One man's eyes did not meet ours when he spoke; he seemed to be choosing his words with great caution. I had a funny feeling he was holding back something.

"Yes, I know—" he answered, "but there is a man in Los Angeles, California, who is helping your sponsors to bring you here to America. It is only polite for you to go thank him. Isn't that the way you were taught to do? Didn't your sponsor teach you some of the ways that we do things here? You see, they spent thousands of dollars to bring you."

Now, here was sense. This was Bwana's order; we could see that plainly. Dona and Bwana always stressed gratitude and politeness to those who did you favors. Dona would not let me wear a thing her friends sent me, no matter how badly I needed it, until I had taken a paper and written a letter of thanks. Dona and Bwana kept sixpence airmail forms in the desk drawer for that very purpose.

Of course we could see sense in saying "Thank you." We knew the original airplane ticket routed our trip from Copenhagen across the North Pole to Los Angeles. But we had thought that making the trip via Los Angeles was some kind of air shortcut. To be in New York already and then fly on to Los Angeles—who could explain a thing like that?

Wearily we picked up our children and walked slowly out to the waiting plane. I believe if Hulme and I had looked at each other we would have burst into a torrent of tears. My nose bled, my legs ached, and my heart hurt.

# 30.

AT LOS ANGELES we wearily descended the stairway from the plane to the pavement. What were we to do? We did not know the name of Dona and Bwana's friend. We wondered where we would eat, where we would sleep, and where I would wash out little Thelma's diapers. She had on her last one, and it probably needed changing. We felt as if even God had forsaken us.

Then suddenly a man in a navy-blue uniform came hurrying toward us. He tried to pronounce our names: "Are you Mr. and Mrs. Si-si-wund-hla?"

Before he got through stammering, our spirits rose. "Yes! Yes!" we cried.

He said he worked for the Trans World Airlines, and a friend by the name of Malmberg had just called and asked him to come meet us. Malmberg was on his way to meet us, but our plane arrived ahead of schedule. We could wait in Malmberg's office. So this was Dona and Bwana's rich friend who brought us to America. He was the one we were to thank. We felt relieved.

At the big, neat office we sank into deep, soft chairs. Our TWA friend ran out to get a stroller so we could push our baby and not have to carry her everywhere. While he was gone, a tall blond man walked into the office. He wore a grin on his face. It was Malmberg!

"Are you Mr. and Mrs. Siwundhla?" he asked, pronouncing our name so correctly that we knew this must be Dona and Bwana's friend.

"My name is Don Malmberg," he said, seizing our hands. "I feel like I know you so well, I'm going to call you Alice and Hulme."

We agreed in chorus, almost feverishly.

"You see, Mr. and Mrs. Edwards and I are good friends. We have a lot in common. She's a writer and so am I. I became interested in their wanting to bring you here."

Mr. Malmberg was so friendly that we felt like we had known him all our lives.

"Now, I'm going to take care of you for the little while you will be here," he assured us.

We began to thank him for all he had done in helping to bring us to America. Why, we would still have been sailing toward Egypt if we had come by boat. It had taken Dona and Bwana weeks to get to America.

He asked us when we had last heard from the Edwardses. We told him we had not had a line for several weeks, and we had missed seeing them in New York City.

He explained that he had made arrangements for them to come to California to meet us there. We got the idea they were driving their car. Ah! That was the answer! They had left New York when we got there!

He packed our luggage into his beautiful car and invited us to get in. His car had little buttons that opened and closed the windows by electricity. These Americans! I thought. How wise and clever they are!

On the way, Mr. Malmberg told us that he was not married, but stayed with his married sister. He wanted to take us to meet his sister first, for she had heard of us and she wanted to see us, too.

We stopped in front of a pretty house and went in. There we saw lovely chairs, flowers, vases, deep rugs, and shining floors. The sister greeted us cordially, and Mr. Malmberg got us some lemonade and ice cream. It was like manna in the desert.

After a while he took us away. "I'm going to let you stay in the home of a friend of ours," he said. "You can rest there until the Edwardses come. I've told the people to get you a good dinner tonight. I know you're hungry!"

We really *were*.

Little Lowell entered the picture just then, "Do you know

Gogo Josalina?" he asked Mr. Malmberg. "I want to see her and big Gogo Lowell."

Don patted him.

"You'll see them, and soon," he assured our eager little boy. The Gogos were known to Lowell only by their pictures and our talk.

At the Malmbergs' house we had seen our first television. Don Malmberg tried to explain it to us, but we did not get too much out of it. Where that picture came from, we could not figure out. It was hard to believe that what we saw was actually happening at that very instant somewhere else.

On the way to the friend's house he pointed out the arrow-like things, which he said were TV antennas, on top of houses. Again we understood nothing.

We stopped at a neat, pretty house, and a Mrs. McIntosh hurried out to the car to meet us. Little Lowell took to her immediately. While we were getting wearily out of the car, the child skipped ahead of us and into the house, and out he ran again. "Mamma!" he cried, "Mamma! Come in! There is a big dish of fruit on the table! Even *nthoci!*" He had found his favorite fruit, the banana, which we had in abundance back home.

"Grapes are there with the bananas, too," he said. A few times we had spent a shilling or two at the European Bakery in Blantyre to buy grapes from the Paarl Valley in South Africa.

We found the home cool and inviting. Our hostess set aside two bedrooms for us, one done in pink and the other in white. Mr. Malmberg left us, promising to come back the next day. He urged us to get a good night of sleep, as Dona and Bwana might pop in at any moment.

We bathed and changed clothes. Mrs. McIntosh tossed our things into her automatic washer, and before we realized it, even Thelma's diapers were dry and folded neatly. These Americans!

When she called us for dinner, we found the table loaded with goodies of every kind.

Mashed potatoes like a drift of snow and running rivers of

melted butter. There were hot biscuits, tender and soft as cotton in the middle, just like Dona taught Andy to make out in Central Africa. Gravy, lima beans, peas, a delectable frosted cake waiting in the tea wagon to be served with ice cream. Hulme's eyes sparkled at the ice cream, his favorite food. After supper we sank into soft chairs in the living room. We watched television for a while, and at last we went to bed.

We awakened the next morning to the smell of hot biscuits and the crackle of frying eggs. After all of our trials and disappointments, after our unnamed fears on the airplane, after wondering if Dona and Bwana had forsaken us, this beautiful home was our happy landing place. It was indeed, "more than we could ask or think," just as the Bible says. We dressed and hurried to the dining room. American cereals in gay, illustrated boxes intrigued little Lowell, and we enjoyed the milk and cream, oatmeal, buttered toast, hot biscuits, syrup, and fresh fruit. Ravenously hungry again, we hardly knew where to begin, or to stop, either.

Mr. Malmberg came to see us the next night, and took us for a long ride. We had seen London and Rome briefly, but Los Angeles seemed larger yet.

He asked us all about the college we wanted to attend. We told him that Bwana and Dona had chosen Oakwood College, at Huntsville, Alabama. She had looked the place over, and it pleased her very much. She thought the climate, not being too severe, might be better for us than a northern school. She had told us that one college refused us point-blank because of little Lowell and Thelma and because of our nationality. But Oakwood had been more than gracious about that.

He seemed so interested in us that I told him a lot of things about our life in Africa, and described Tillie and Camie, my sister and brother. I told him, too, that because of our training from Bwana and Dona we were glad to come all the way from New York to California to thank him for helping us. We explained that it was a strong African custom to return thanks no matter how small the favor.

Then, as he drove us about in his fine car, he asked us how we would like to see ourselves on television. I stared at him unbelievingly. "Is that possible?" I asked.

"I have friends in the TV business," he answered. "I think we might do that just for fun, while we're waiting for your folks to come from New York. I'll see if I can arrange it. Then when you write to your friends in Africa, you can say you have not only seen television, but you have actually seen yourselves on TV."

Hulme and I had to ponder that for a while. So many unbelievable things had happened already, that if he had told us the folk in Los Angeles had found out that the moon was a big Edam cheese, we would have thought he was telling the truth. Our little boy, too, trusted our new friend, and wanted always to sit by him in the house or in the car.

We loved Don because he made us feel important. Hulme and I agreed that Dona and Bwana attracted wonderful friends because they themselves were wonderful.

Bwana had always told us that every person is important, not just rich people. Life is sacred, and even a "little" person has his right to get ahead and have happiness. He taught us that this belief is really democracy. He used lovely words. He called it the intrinsic worth of every individual. Don, too, was a real American: He lived democracy.

On the way home Don got us some kind of orange drink. And he made us practice counting American money so no one would take advantage of us when we bought things by ourselves.

"You will need to know this," he said. "You are going to be here in America for several years. You might as well begin to learn now."

# 31.

WHEN we got back to the house that night, we went to bed, but we got up hungry again at two in the morning. We could not get straightened up in our day and night. We made big sandwiches and wrote some more letters. We wanted to go and mail the letters the next morning, but Mrs. McIntosh took us in her car. For some reason our new friends didn't want us to go anywhere by ourselves. We decided they didn't wish us to get lost or hurt in the heavy traffic.

The next afternoon Don came with a friend, a quiet, dark-complexioned young man named Mr. Dick Gottlieb. This man asked us all kinds of questions, though he seemed to know the answers already. He asked us why we came to America. Of course, we waxed voluble on that! He inquired about the mission station and our life there, and we told him of our marriage and praised the many virtues of Bwana and Dona. I told him also about my brave sister Tillie, and about my brother Cameron, what they were doing and where they lived. I talked a stream, and poor Hulme sat there in his quiet way and did not slip in a word between all of mine. He is like Bwana in that way. When Dona and I were together, Bwana would sit and chuckle and say we were alike as twin calves!

We had turned the television down, so little Lowell pulled up a footstool and watched it. Little Thelma lay on a blanket, teething and drooling, her baby eyes also fixed on the flickering picture.

Mr. Gottlieb—Dick, as he wanted us to call him—asked more questions about Africa, Dona, Bwana, Malamulo, Luwazi, Gogo, and Nkata Bay. I guess I gabbled like a duck, I was so full of talk.

I told him our love story, and how Dona and Bwana felt that God had brought us together in a special way.

Hulme had such high ideals, after he became a Christian, I said, and he was also a great dreamer. He had hopes for a life higher than the other men of his village. I tried to explain this to Mr. Dick Gottlieb while Hulme just sat there, his mouth curved up in a smile, his dark eyes mellow with remembering.

I told how Hulme had been teased by his boss in Cape Town, Pastor Cardey.

"Sir," Hulme had said, "I have a dream of an ideal girl."

"A dream girl? Be realistic, Hulme! What kind of girl?"

"First, wise, educated, clever."

"You're narrowing your field pretty rigidly, Son."

"That's not all. I want her to be pretty, able to sew and cook, with a nice personality, too."

"There is no such girl!" insisted practical Pastor Cardey. "You can't find all of those accomplishments in one girl!"

Here Hulme interrupted Dick and me:

"My room seemed so lonely and so meaningless," he explained. "When I came home, no one was there to meet me, to greet me and welcome me. I had a small electric stove, and prepared my own food, and sewed on my own buttons, and did my own cleaning. But it was lonely."

"But you didn't weaken?" queried Dick.

"Not for a moment," Hulme answered. Then he lowered his voice. "You see, Mr. Gottlieb, I had a strange dream. It was so different, I thought it must come true. You see, I believe in prayer. I began to pray for a wife.

"It was strange. I didn't see anything, but a voice, sweet and musical, spoke to me, and said, 'Do not worry, Hulme. I have chosen you a wife from a far country.'" He laughed. "That is why I named her Star, *Inkwekwezi*, on our wedding day, because she came from a far country."

I went on telling Mr. Dick all about how Dona and Bwana got us so interested in college, and in getting ready to be of service to our people. "'You don't know how wonderful college is!' Bwana used to say. 'I worked my whole way. I worked cruelly hard, but it was wonderful just the same. Dona helped me. She taught school and wrote stories and poems and sold them, and wore old made-over clothes. But nothing is hard if it is a labor of love.'

"A labor of love, Mr. Dick," I told him fervently, "that is what Mother and Father Edwards have been doing for us, and for Africa all the years. And don't think even the heathen in our country don't know it! I have heard them talk about them, and they call Bwana 'Wacifundo' (merciful one), too, just as the Christians do."

I might have been talking to Mr. Gottlieb still, but he and Don had to go. I had just gotten steamed up and would have liked to go on and on and on.

Later Don came back and took us to see the mighty Pacific Ocean. Now we had seen our third ocean. He took us everywhere—through tunnels, over bridges, to the airport, to a place where they made fertilizer, and everywhere we looked were colored neon lights winking. Our eyes so used to darkness and our ears accustomed to silence had to turn somersaults to adjust to the sights and sounds of America.

On the way back, Don spoke to Hulme.

"Dick wants to talk to you tomorrow. He wants to get you alone, as he heard your wife's side of the story today. Then there are some African customs he wants to ask you about. I am coming around noon to take you there. Is that all right?"

Hulme assured him this was the least he could do for all the kindness showered upon us.

# 32.

*I* WAS in the bedroom putting little Thelma to sleep after lunch the next day when Mr. Malmberg came again to see us. Hulme was, of course, watching television in the living room. We were still so intrigued with it that we could hardly let it alone.

Don asked Hulme to go with him and talk to Mr. Dick Gottlieb in his office. He said he had to get Hulme away from me so they could hear what Hulme had to say. I laughed, remembering Bwana's joke about Dona and me: "English is the mother tongue. Father doesn't get to use it."

He told me to get a good rest that afternoon. "I think I've got it almost worked out," he said, "so you can see yourselves on television. I might get it worked out for tonight."

He patted my shoulder, smiled his big smile, and left with Hulme.

At five that afternoon Mrs. McIntosh awakened me from my nap. I ran to the mirror and rubbed cream on my face and straightened my hair. I had on a gored skirt and a sweater I had knitted. It was a pretty cerise color with an intricate pattern. She told me that Mr. Don Malmberg was already there waiting for me, and I should get ready to go with him. He might be in a hurry.

When I met him, I asked him where Hulme was. "I just got so busy in my office, Alice, that I did not have time to go get him," he explained.

"My land!" I cried. "He had no American money. How could he get anything to eat?"

"Mr. Gottlieb won't let Hulme starve," laughed Don. "We don't do things like that in America!"

I told Don I would go press a dress and comb my hair, and I would be ready soon.

"You're all right," he said, expansively. "Don't worry. I've got it all worked out for you to see yourself on television, and you look just fine. We don't have too much time. Traffic is heavy, and it will take us quite a while to get to the studio."

I changed Thelma, and took one extra diaper and a nursing bottle. Soon, in Don's red car, we wound through the heavy traffic of the Los Angeles freeways. I was a little surprised that Mrs. McIntosh and another lady went with us.

"She wants to watch you tonight when you see yourself on television," Don explained. I was aghast. Was this to be such an event? And here I was, not even dressed up. What would Dona say if she should see me on television in an old sweater and skirt?

Quite suddenly I began to be fearful of something, I knew not what. Dona would have called it intuition or premonition. I began to feel a little numb about this whole thing. Maybe I'd been foolish to promise to do this.

"How far is this place? Where will we see ourselves on television? If it's such an occasion, maybe you should have let me get dressed up a little, sir."

Don just laughed.

"You're all right," he said. "That's a pretty sweater. It will look nice on TV." Then he changed the subject and began to point out how people were already putting up Christmas trees and other decorations. After a while we drove into a huge parking area, and the attendants there acted as if they knew Don. I was not surprised, because he was so friendly he must have made friends everywhere. They let him park very near the building, in what looked to me like a special place.

"Do you know what N.B.C. stands for?" he asked casually as we got out. Ah! here was something I knew.

"Does it mean the Nyasaland Tobacco Corporation?" I asked, really confused.

He laughed heartily at that, and I felt chagrined at my ignorance. But he set me at my ease right away.

"No, no," he said. "This is the place where you will see yourself on television. There are several of these places. This one is called N.B.C., which means National Broadcasting Company. I decided to take you to this one, for I know a man here who is going to let you see yourself. He is very kind, and you will like him. Hulme is already here!"

By that time I saw the big entrance to the building, and it looked as if thousands of people were milling around, waiting to get in. My curiosity was aroused. Why would those Americans have to stand out there and wait, while I, a foreigner, could enter by this back way so easily?

Don told me to wait while he took little Lowell to the rest room. That was logical, for I knew the importance of little things like that.

When he came back, he looked as innocent as a cat who had just taken his paw out of a goldfish bowl.

"Sir," I said, "what are all those people waiting for out there? I asked Mrs. McIntosh, and she said you'd be sure to know."

Don had come back without little Lowell. He looked at me a little queerly, I thought. "Those people have come to see you when you see yourself on television," he said shortly. I almost stopped breathing. He reached into the car and took little Thelma, who gave him a toothless smile.

"Sir," I protested, "I'm feeling a little sick. I have a stomach-ache and a headache, so maybe we had better wait till another day."

"Oh, you'll be all right," he assured me airily. "Come along. I want you to meet the man who agreed to let you see yourself on TV. His name is Edwards, but he is not your Bwana. He wants to ask you a few things about Africa."

"But, sir," I said, "Africa is a very large continent, and there are many things I do not know about it. And besides, most of what I know I have read out of geography books. You can't travel much over there."

But Don only laughed as we walked along a hall with closed doors.

We paused in front of an imposing mahogany door. "Alice, do not be afraid," Don said. "You will not be afraid of Mr. Ralph

Edwards. He is as nice as your Bwana Edwards, and you will feel very much at home with him."

He opened the door, and we stepped in. The room seemed to me to be filled with big, tall men all looking right at me. Hulme sat with little Lowell on his knee, but he hardly looked at me. That scared me a little. Was he angry at me about something?

A pleasant man stepped up to me and took my hand, putting me at ease immediately.

"I am Ralph Edwards," he told me. "You must be the Alice I have heard so much about. I'm just going to call you Alice, since I feel like I already know you."

I was a little disarmed by his pleasant manner, but was still afraid I might be showing up my ignorance when he got to asking me questions.

I saw Mr. Gottlieb there and a big man whose name, I learned, was Axel Gruenwald.

Ralph Edwards said, "Now, Alice, I have a few questions I would like to ask you about Africa. You see, Africa is coming into the news more and more these days, and it is a privilege to have someone who is from there who can tell us all about the things we'd like to know."

My tongue felt stiff as a mealie cob in my mouth, I was so frightened. I looked up at him as appealing as I knew how.

"I'm not an authority on Africa, sir," I said in a low, weak voice. "My knowledge is so limited; you are sure to be disappointed."

"The questions are easy," he said. "You're sure to know them. But you're just not to worry."

I sneaked another look at Hulme. He didn't seem at all pleased or excited about seeing me, and in his face was a look I could not read. Was it fear? Had we walked into some kind of trap here where Dona and Bwana could not protect us?

Then Mr. Ralph Edwards left the room for a moment and returned with his tie and coat on, as if dressed up for some big event. He had a red book in his hand with a white paper clipped to it.

"Alice," he said, "here are those easy questions. Now let's go into the other room." He invited Hulme to come along, too.

When we came to a corner, he stopped and said, "Now, Alice, there will be many people in the seats in this place, and also cameras on wheels, and men who will be wanting to take a picture of you for television. Don't pay any attention to them. They may come near to your face, but they won't hurt you. Act as if you don't even see them. Just look at me and listen to me. This is the way we take pictures on television."

I was terror-stricken. The thing was so complicated and stupendous. What had I let myself in for? I looked frantically around for some way to escape, but saw none. Everyone in the world seemed to be looking right at us.

In front of us was a couch, something like Dona bought us for our sitting room in Africa. In front of it was a coffee table with a flower arrangement on it. The place was gorgeous, but it frightened me more than when a lion scratched at our door at Mwami Mission.

He told us to sit down. Then he told the audience that here was a family who had traveled to America all the way from the very heart of Africa to be on this program. Then he turned and looked straight at me. A camera wheeled in close.

"Alice Princess Siwundhla," he said in his clear voice, "This Is Your Life!"

My heart skipped. Was he going to take my life? What had I done to deserve death? We had seen people shoot and kill people on television at Mrs. McIntosh's house. The only thing I could think of was to smile up at him. Maybe if I acted pleasant enough he would forgive me, and I could only hope he would not shoot Hulme, too. The children needed someone to take care of them in case I was killed.

"Alice," he continued, "do you have any idea what 'This Is Your Life' is?"

"No, sir," I answered, a little relieved. "No, I don't."

"It is a program on television, Alice, and right now people all over America are watching you. We are going to take you back to Africa now; not really, but in memory. How long have you been in America?" he asked.

"Only three days," I answered. It seemed like three years.

"Have you ever seen television before?" he asked.

"Only since we have been in America," I answered. "The missionaries tried to explain it to us, but it was so complicated we couldn't understand a thing about it."

Just then little Lowell spied us in the monitor screen.

"Mamma! Mamma!" he shouted, laughing and jumping. "There we are! There we are on television! Look at me, Lowell," he cried, addressing the little boy on the screen.

Ralph Edwards laughed at that, and so did the audience off in the darkness behind the rolling, wheeling cameras.

# 33.

"WELL, let's take that trip to Africa—here on the stage, of course," Ralph Edwards continued. "We are going to tell America the story of your life; from the mud and dung-covered floor of the hut of your childhood, among the people of upper Nyasaland, to this night and this seat, where the great and the small of our land have been honored—but never one who has come so far in miles and in mental and social adjustment as *you*—Alice Siwundhla."

He struggled manfully over that last name, but he said it correctly. Then he turned his eyes from me, and a burst of applause filled the room.

"Ladies and gentlemen," he said, "we will soon span oceans and continents to tell the story of a little girl who grew up in the stark reality of a primitive African village . . . and who today has her eyes on a college education in America."

While Bob Warren came in with a commercial about that time, Ralph explained it to me. He told me that if it were not for a sponsor called *Prell* they could not have spent all these thousands of dollars to bring us to America, and to tell our story before millions of people.

He had had Hulme and the children occupy some seats behind us. And there I sat all alone facing this great man. I knew he must be a great man; he had to be to wield such power!

"Now we are going to start at the beginning of your story, turn the clock backward, spin the globe from Los Angeles, California, to Johannesburg, South Africa."

There on the monitor in front of me, magically enough, was a globe. It whirled and stopped, pinpointing the golden city of my birth. My, I was relieved by that time. No pistol shots to mow me and my family down!

146

"Only six days ago, Alice Siwundhla and her family boarded a plane in Salisbury, Southern Rhodesia, Africa, traveled to Nairobi, Khartoum, Rome, London, and on to Los Angeles, California, so that we can say a phrase that all America knows, and that you will understand as the evening goes on. Tonight, Alice Siwundhla, this is your life!"

Now I looked at this man in great wonder. I knew Americans were clever people. We had concluded that long ago in Africa. But how could this man whom I had never seen before know so much about my life fifteen minutes after I had been introduced to him? This seemed like *mfiti*, witchcraft.

Then I had a horrible thought. If he was a magician who used some kind of machine to fetch back the past, he could see some of my dirty tricks and meanness and mistakes. Oh, dear! Just what had he seen? And what was he fixing to tell those millions of folk all over America about me? I ought to get him aside somehow and tell him not to tell about how stubborn I was, and how I had hurt Bwana and Dona by disobeying them. No use to tell that.

"The more you stir a stink the worse it smells," Dona and Bwana always said, and they were great forgivers. But I was caught, and had no time for a single word alone with him. Those old cameras wheeled back and forth like white ants flying out of a hole.

"Your first memories, Alice," he continued, "are probably not of the filth and the flies and the superstitions of the village up near lake Nyasa, deep in Africa, that was almost to entrap you as a young girl. That will come after you are six years old when you had to return to the heathen village of your father's people.

"Here in Johannesburg you are born in a neat little brick house, close to the City Deep Hospital. You live with your dear mother, Lena Mbombo Msumba, and your father, Akim Msumba, your older sister, Mathilda, and your baby brother, Cameron."

How could he know all those names? How did he know about the City Deep, and baby Camie and sister Tillie? These Americans! But I must listen carefully so I could shush him up if he said too much.

"Your father as a young man came to Johannesburg from his native village to find work. There he met your mother, the lovely Lena Mbombo, who was a nurse. Was your father a Christian, Alice?"

"Oh, yes," I said. "He went to the Church of England."

"Your father was attracted to your mother because she was different from the girls he had known back in Nyasaland. The girls there made themselves attractive by taking sharp stones and cutting designs into the skin of their bodies. Into the cuts they would rub ground-up charcoal to make the scars plainly visible. Many would file their front teeth and stretch and elongate their upper and lower lips."

I wondered where he had read all these things about my father's tribe. Dear, dear! There were some heathen customs I hoped he hadn't seen in his crystal ball.

"Do girls still do this in Nyasaland?" he asked me.

"Oh, yes, some do. But those who accept Christianity try to do away with it."

"But your mother had escaped from these tribal customs," he continued, "and so she had a clear, smooth skin. And she had curtains on the windows of your little home, and beds with linen, and good food."

Tears came to my eyes as the dear memories came flooding back, memories of love and care and kisses, and providence, and fresh-baked bread with butter and jam.

"There, near the hospital in Johannesburg, the happy days in your young life pass all too quickly. And one night your mother comes home from the hospital, overtired and overworked, with pneumonia. Death comes suddenly in Africa, and that very night she passes away. Your father, with a great grief in his heart, tries to carry on. He tries to raise you and your brother and sister in the Christian way of life. But he works too hard and grieves too much. Within a year, he breaks down with consumption."

Then, from some kind of speaker, I heard the strangest thing. I could have sworn it was Tillie's (Mathilda's) voice. My sister, in her peculiar high Cinyanja and Citumbuka voice, was plainly talking to me from out of the air. No one talks quite like Mathilda. My admiration for Americans grew still more. Imitating my Tillie so exactly! How could they?

"Our father decided," said the voice, "that it would be best if we all returned to his native village where the weather was warm and the air was warm and clear."

"Alice," Ralph said, "I told you you would meet some people who were important to you. Do you know who that could be?"

"My sister, Mathilda," I answered.

"Your sister, Mathilda, two years older than you. Are you surprised to hear her voice?"

"Yes," I said. "It can't be, for she is in Africa."

"No, Alice, she is right here, just a few steps away. You see, that is the way our television show works.

"This is your life, Alice. Come out, Sister Mathilda, flown here from Luwazi Mission!"

I looked around wildly, no longer able to trust my ears or my eyes. A feather could have pushed me off that divan onto the floor.

Suddenly there she was, in a pink *nsaru* just as they wore them back at Luwazi, with little David on her back. She stretched out her arms to encompass me, and I ran to her. We wept out loud, not caring a bit if 40,000,000 people were watching us. My darling Tillie who had been sister and mother and father to me for so long!

When Ralph Edwards could be heard, he said, almost gaily, "And look who she has with her! Her little son, David, your nephew. And do you know, he flew, too, to America."

They had a hard time quieting Tillie and me. I can't tell you what we were crying about, unless it was because the old heartbreaks and loneliness had been made so vivid in our memory. Umame's death, and Tata's, too—old wounds we had thought were healed were bleeding afresh; and the lights, and wheeling cameras, and strangers over there on those tiers of seats added to the tension. Then, the element of utter amazement!

I honestly thought they were through with us then, and I could hardly wait to get Tillie off in some corner and ask her how *she* ever got to Hollywood. I started walking away with Tillie, but Ralph Edwards would not let me go. He told Sister Mathilda and little David to go back there where Hulme was sitting with a mysterious smile on his face. Ah, he knew something I didn't know, the rascal!

"You stay here, Alice," Ralph said. "We have a few more things for you to know, and a few more surprises."

Just then I heard another familiar voice say, "We three children were left alone; Mathilda was eleven, Alice was eight, and I was six."

"Alice," Ralph said to me, "there's the voice of someone who is very close to you, too."

It was Cameron's voice. Maybe Cameron really was there, unless I was dreaming.

"It *is* your brother, indeed. It is Cameron, flown here from the Solusi Training School, Bulawayo, Southern Rhodesia. He has come to share your life with you tonight!"

Cameron materialized, indeed! He gave me a big kiss and a hug, and then he sat down as cool as an ice cube from Dona's paraffin refrigerator and began to answer Ralph's questions as if he had been in America all his life.

"Cameron, would you tell us what happened in your village after your father died?"

Cameron calmly answered, "As soon as the people found out what had happened, Mr. Edwards, they came into our hut and took out everything, even the blanket which covered our father's body."

"How was your health out there, Cameron?"

Cameron's face clouded as he told of malaria and dysentery and viciously biting flies and how he had been carried so far away from Tillie and me that we never expected to meet again in this world.

Then Ralph told Cameron to sit with Hulme, Thelma, Lowell, Tillie, and David. I was alone again, looking up quizzically into the face of Mr. This-Is-Your-Life.

"Alice," he said, "as the pulse of your life goes on in your village, how those drums change into the sweetness of bells!"

A picture of the pretty brick church back at the Malamulo Mission flashed onto the monitor screen. That was one of Bwana's pictures! I had seen it many times.

Then the commercial flashed on. *Prell* shampoo. It did so much for me, we've all used it ever since. It would seem like heresy, blackmail, arson, and bigamy to use anything but *Prell*, or *Lilt*, or *Crest*.

Suddenly the commercial stopped, and I saw myself and Ralph on the nearby monitor. Ralph turned to me.

"Well, now, let's get back to 'This Is Your Life.' From your village, Alice, you can hear the bells of Luwazi Mission ringing loud and clear. You and Mathilda remember the sound of the church bells from Johannesburg. You remember how your mother and father would take you to church services in Johannesburg, and how you would sing hymns, and the church would be cool and clean and quiet. Alice, you and Mathilda go to where the bells are ringing, even though you were told not to do so."

Did this man have some kind of magic machine that could suck up images from the past? If so, he could see lots of unsavory things. He would see how Mathilda laughed at my toes and teeth, and how she said my eyebrows joined, looking like the baboon's. I had run screaming to Umame and Tata to beat her for that—to beat her hard. Wasn't I a *princess?* Wasn't I named for Princess Alice, the sister of the king of England? Funny how thoughts can run with the speed of a cheetah. I thought all that while Mr. Edwards paused for only an instant.

Then I heard another voice, the voice of dear Mrs. Lydia Davy, who had befriended us at Luwazi Mission. The voice said,

"I saw two little children in dresses far too small for them, sitting in the church. I just had to talk with them afterward."

"Do you know who that is?" asked Ralph.

By now I was callous to miracles. "That's Mrs. Davy."

"And they are important in your life, Alice?" he asked. "Come

Alice happily dries a tear as Pastor and Mrs. Ludlow Davy suddenly appear on the stage with Ralph Edwards in "This Is Your Life" TV program. The Davys found Alice and her sister at Luwazi Mission.

in, Pastor and Mrs. W. L. Davy of Luwazi Mission, Nyasaland!"

From that mysterious door they came, smiling, and we all wept and hugged each other again.

"Mrs. Davy," said Ralph, "tell us what happened when you talked to Alice and Mathilda after the services."

"The girls told me they were orphans. Of course I asked them if they were going to school. They said their people had told them no man would marry them if they went to school, because no man likes an educated girl."

How well I knew about that!

"I went to see the chief of their village," Mr. Davy added, "and I asked him to let the girls come to Luwazi to school. Yes, sir," boomed Pastor Davy in his decisive voice, "I said, 'Now those girls have got to be in school, and that's all there is to it!'"

Ralph had Mr. and Mrs. Davy go back and sit with the rest. I wondered, "What next?" when I heard a familiar musical voice.

"Do you recognize that voice, Alice?" Ralph asked.

"Yes!" I was smiling broadly. "Mrs. Ruth Phillips." I almost said "Nyafilipo," for that was our pet name for her.

"It belongs to a very good friend of yours," he said, "one of your teachers at the Malamulo Mission School. She now lives at Lacombe, Alberta, Canada. Come in, Mrs. Ruth Phillips!"

That door! How eagerly I watched for dear Mrs. Phillips, whose fingers were so full of music. She had played Dona's piano for my wedding march, and she sang like an angel. She and Dona had loved to conjure up tricks together and then laugh till they cried.

"Was Alice a good student in school, Mrs. Phillips?"

"Oh, yes, she was, Mr. Edwards. She became an expert seamstress, she learned English quickly, and she learned to play the piano. She is a good cook and a wonderful housekeeper."

"Did Alice talk to you about marriage, Mrs. Phillips?"

Mrs. Phillips smiled at the memory.

"Yes. You see, the African customs are different from ours. I told Alice that marriage and the marriage ceremony should be and is a happy affair. But among the Africans of that area, it is con-

sidered wrong for a girl to smile at her marriage. A smiling girl
is a bad girl!"

With that Ralph turned back to Hulme, who was sitting back
of us, holding Thelma on his lap.

"Did Alice smile at your wedding, Hulme?"

The cameras panned in on my husband until his face filled the
whole screen.

"Oh, yes!" he answered. "All the time!"

The audience behind the cameras and the lights buzzed with
apparent delight.

# 34.

ONE thing bothered me. What had happened to Dona and Bwana? Where were they? I began to feel as if a great wrong had been done, when Ralph started talking again.

"Here at Malamulo, a Seventh-day Adventist mission, Alice, you not only became friends with Mrs. Phillips, but you came under the guidance and love of two people who actually have been a second mother and father to you—Mr. and Mrs. Lowell Edwards."

Suddenly a weight as heavy as a hippo fell off my mind. Little tremors began to run through me, and my eyes strained at that partition! Oh, dear Lord God in heaven, who showers blessings like the Chiperoni rains on my head, are they there? So many years had passed since that day in Limbe when the train tore our hands apart and we heard their tender sobs. Their faces were etched in our hearts when we could see them no more!

But they did not come out. I strained my eyes in vain. But, oh dear! Ralph had that "back in the past" machine wound up and working again. Of all things, he began talking about my boy-friends. I had kept still about things like that, for Dona's and Bwana's prayers had found me my own dear Hulme, who was sitting back there smiling his secret smile.

"Did you have any offers of marriage, Alice?" Ralph asked.

My heart turned cold. Could that machine see all the winnowing baskets full of marriage offers from Mtali, Bwani, Fort Hill, the Rhodesias, Mozambique, Chiromo, Tanganyika, Uganda, and even the Union of South Africa? I looked up at Ralph a little fearfully and answered as bravely as I could. "Yes, sir," I said, so low that I hoped those cameramen and the mob back of the lights could not hear me.

"We know, Alice," he continued, "that you accepted none until

At last Pastor and Mrs. Lowell Edwards appeared on the stage, and the reunion was complete.

Hulme proposed. But one such offer comes in a letter from an African young man who had seen you at the time of Mathilda's wedding. You gaze at the handsome photograph he encloses, and you get excited when he tells you he is coming to see you from his native village."

How on earth did he dig this out, unless he used that magic machine?

"On this very night the handsome young man comes to see you and, dressed in your best dress, you go to meet him."

My heart pained at that, for in my disloyalty I had actually worn a dress Dona's loving hands had given me.

"What did he ask you to do, Alice? What did he tell you?"

"That if I would run off with him and marry him, he would give me many things," I whispered.

"As he talks to you there, you remember the counsels of your father who, lying at death's door, told you to be a God-fearing child and never be taken in by greed and selfishness. You tell your young man to come back for his answer tomorrow. But, Alice, you are bewildered and hurt by a false accusation of theft, and you are faced with a choice between Christianity and a heathen marriage. So you return to the mission in tears."

Suddenly I heard the sweet voice I had been longing to hear. "That Sunday afternoon," the voice said, "up the hill at the mission house, I had a premonition that all was not well with my Alice, that she was in trouble—"

Then Bwana's kind voice, so gentle and tender, continued, "My wife got on her bicycle and went down immediately to see what might be wrong."

I looked up at Ralph, and my face must have radiated some of the joy I felt surging in my heart, for he said, "Well, Alice, no need to tell you who those people are, is there? The couple who looked after you in Africa, and who are directly responsible for your being here tonight, Mr. and Mrs. Lowell A. Edwards of New York City!"

In ran Dona and Bwana. They enveloped me, they hugged me,

they cried. For once in her life Dona could hardly speak. Bwana had to laugh at that, for he always said she had something to say about everything. But she gulped and sobbed, and little Lowell shrilled out, "Gogo Josalina," and the tears streamed down Bwana's cheeks, and mine, and even Hulme's.

After a while we got through hugging and squeezing and crying and laughing. I knew they still loved me just as if I were their same color, and just as if they didn't know a lot of mean things I had done.

Ralph Edwards had to interrupt us and remind us that over 40,000,000 people still wanted to see the television program. He got us settled down at last, and began talking again.

"You turn your back on heathen marriage, Alice, and spend the remaining years of the Edwardses' stay in Africa with them. While with them on their furlough in Cape Town, you met Hulme."

Hulme came out with little Thelma in his arms and said, "Yes, I was a printer in Cape Town. We fell in love, became engaged, and were married June 17, 1952. This was at the Malamulo Mission, where I became a monotype operator for the mission press."

I looked at Hulme. How did *he* get in on this? How long since he knew all about it? How could he keep so many secrets from me?

Ralph turned back to that lovely couple with hearts of pure gold. "Ever since you left Africa, Mr. and Mrs. Edwards, you have saved every penny you could rake and scrape together to bring Alice and Hulme to the United States."

Bwana, in his kindly, mellow voice, answered, "Yes, Mr. Edwards. With a college education here in America, they can go back to their people and help them to rise above ignorance and superstition as Alice and Hulme have done."

Then I looked at Dona, waiting for her to speak. We had already greeted each other and cried all over that part of the studio, but I stood feasting my eyes on the dearest people on God's earth.

Dona said, "We feel very proud that they named their oldest son Lowell, after my husband, and their daughter Thelma, after me."

Ralph Edwards, "This Is Your Life" master of ceremonies, chats with the Siwundhlas.

Then Ralph said into the microphone, "Ladies and gentlemen, we received a letter from Mrs. Edwards here, telling us .the story of Alice. We became so interested in Alice's life that we asked Mrs. Edwards if we might be a part of the great work they are doing. In just a moment, Alice and Hulme, and Mr. and Mrs. Edwards, we would humbly like to take that part."

Fortunately, commercials came in every little bit. We had a chance to grab each other and try to comprehend the marvel and miracle that had happened to us. The announcer talked about *Crest* toothpaste, I remember, but whether it helped soft spots on the head or on the teeth, I could not have told if a gun had been pointed at me. I only know that since then, there is only one kind of toothpaste for us, for it helped Dona and Bwana and Ralph to move mountains.

"And now, Alice," Ralph said, "let's see what the future holds in store for you and your family. First of all, Marchal Jewelers of New York City have custom-designed for you this beautiful gold charm bracelet. Each of the charms is a lasting reminder of some important event in your life."

He laid in my hands a purple velvet-lined jewel box, in which lay the most gorgeous thing. A tiny gold lamp stood for education, and a replica of Dona and Bwana's house in gold hung by a tiny chain. You could open the roof upon a hinge and see golden furniture inside. A little car with moving wheels and even a trunk (*boot*, we call it in Africa) stood for the memorable coastal furlough. The wedding bell had a clapper made of a ruby; a tiny scuffed shoe laced with rubies and garnets reminded us of baby Lowell's birth, and a pram symbolized Thelma. Then, oh, dear, a map of Africa with a diamond at Johannesburg, my birthplace, and a golden calendar leaf, 1956, November. A diamond gleamed out from Wednesday, November 28—the date of the television program.

In Africa polite people do not receive a gift with one hand—they hold out both hands. So I received that lovely golden gift in my two hands.

Alice Siwundhla and "Dona" Edwards, her second mother.

I have not told nearly all the things that gleamed and glittered from that golden band, such as the tiny golden book with three pages, representing the postal savings book our Tata left for us, trying so hard in his illness to provide for us.

Then the tiny piano made me remember the hours Dona hung over me, teaching me to play the hymns for church services. The first piece of music I learned was "The Merry Farmer." My, that was hard, but she did not rest till I had learned it well.

Marchal Jewelers sent me a letter with this lovely bracelet, which I shall ever cherish:

"Dear Mrs. Siwundhla:

"We have been commissioned by Mr. Ralph Edwards to design and create a 14 karat gold charm bracelet, representing many of the thrilling and important events in your life.

"We sincerely hope that this bracelet will bring you many years of pleasure.

Cordially,

Marchal, Inc.

Charles H. Fleishman."

They gave wristwatches to Cameron, dear Mathilda, and Hulme. Tillie had needed a watch for her teaching work at Luwazi Mission, and she had never owned one in her life. What a thrill for her! These watches were from *Prell*, the most wonderful shampoo in the world. Try it if you don't believe it. It not only cleans your hair, but it flies people above the clouds across the world to Hollywood.

We got a beautiful Bell and Howell projector and movie camera, and best of all, a film of the telecast of my life. Now I could share this "dream come true" with other people.

I knew, for Dona and Bwana had told us, that Oakwood College in Huntsville, Alabama, had accepted us. But life in America with its different houses and foods and streets and clothes and habits seemed so bewilderingly different that I wondered if Hulme and I would make it at college. We seemed like two tiny peanuts

Lively youngsters, Lowell and Thelma, as they
appeared upon arrival in the United States.

sitting there. How could we fit into anything American, when everything is fabulous in America if it is American at all?

But Ralph confidently said, "Now, Alice, we know that Mr. and Mrs. Edwards here have already enrolled you at Oakwood College, and they have arranged a comfortable little apartment for you and your family. You are going to take them there and see that they are settled, aren't you, Mr. and Mrs. Edwards?"

"Yes, we are," Dona answered, laying her hand on my shoulder.

"Now, Alice Princess Siwundhla," Ralph went on, "because your life has been told tonight, Mr. and Mrs. Edwards have been able to save the $1,000 they planned to spend for your fare from Africa. Now they can add that to the money they already had saved up for your education. Mr. and Mrs. Edwards here are wonderful examples of man's humanity to man. Ladies and gentlemen, missionaries are wonderful people!"

How proud I was that millions of people could know of the multitude of good things Pastor and Mrs. Edwards had done.

How can I tell of the money Ralph Edwards and *Prell* and *Crest* and others sent to Oakwood? Of Spiegel's helping us with $500 more? Of the $1,000 for food that Mr. Don Grimes, president of 6,000 I.G.A. stores, gave us? Or of the $6,000 worth of medicine sent to Malamulo Mission Hospital in my name?

After the great program, "This Is Your Life" held a party in the Hollywood Roosevelt Hotel. Both Dona and Bwana were kept so busy they could scarcely eat, for telephone calls came from all over the United States. You never saw such a party. Bwana was so pleased that he thanked the chef in person. That is like Bwana.

There we met Bwana's oldest son, who is the image of his father. We had seen his pictures many times, for he sings first tenor in the King's Heralds Quartet, of the Voice of Prophecy radiobroadcast. Hulme had worked for that organization in Cape Town, so he was overjoyed to meet our dear brother Bob. He, with his wife, Irene, had been invited to the party. Like *Wacifundo,* his father, he welcomed me to the family.

After the fabulous party at the Hollywood Roosevelt Hotel, we

The Siwundhla family today. Left to right: Lowell, Ralph (born in America and named after Ralph Edwards), Thelma, Hulme, and Alice.

visited some places of interest, and in a few days we rode with Dona and Bwana to our apartment at Oakwood College. There they welcomed us. But the greatest joy was getting home. We had gone to get some things, and while we were gone, Dona had put a pot of soup on the stove and a pan of corn bread in the oven. We tramped up the stairs and opened the door of our new home, so neat and so clean.

Hulme stopped. "Oh, honey," he said, "we are home. We can rest now, and food is cooking, and Mother is here." I could have wept for joy at that.

Here we met another brother, Charles Edwards, and his wife, June. He is big, tall, and friendly, and as sweet as his parents. He is a minister, like Bwana.

Five months later a little American came to join us, and he surprised Dona and Bwana both, and Ralph Edwards, too, as we wanted to surprise him. He was a little hitchhiker on the plane from Africa to America. For whom could we name our babe?

Well, he is a sturdy little boy of eight now, and he bears the name of Ralph Edwards—Ralph Edwards Siwundhla.

He has never seen Africa, but he will, God willing, when we go back to do the work Bwana and Dona prepared us to do.

# POSTSCRIPT

MANY friends have asked me why I stopped the story at this point. They want to know what experiences we have had during the past several years, since we came to the United States. My answer is that there is much to tell; but to relate all that has happened would have made this book too long.

As to what I have been doing, I'm very busy and happy with what God has provided for us. After our TV appearance we attended Oakwood College, where I earned my B.A. in Business Administration. I then entered an M.A. program at California State Polytechnic College in San Luis Obispo, where I received my degree in Education while Hulme worked on his Ph.D. at the University of California in Santa Barbara. Now I am also studying at Santa Barbara, so our family is together again.

Being a housewife and mother of three children, attending university classes, and encouraging my husband with his studies— all of this is a full-time occupation. But in addition, churches, clubs, and many other organizations up and down the Pacific Coast and across the country have invited me to speak before them. Thousands of people who have heard our story have been most kind and appreciative.

In spite of this busy schedule, I plan to write another book, in which I'll tell about our exciting adventures in the United States. Sometime, somehow, this sequel will be completed.

# Glossary

Foreign words and phrases used are mostly in Cinyanja and Xhosa, but a few are British or Afrikaans colloquialisms.

| | | | |
|---|---|---|---|
| *Akristu* | Christian | *ng'anga* | sweetheart |
| *bushveld* | grassy prairie | *nkhoswe* | marriage arranger |
| *bwana* | mister, form of respect | *nkuku* | chicken |
| *Bwerani* | Come here | *nsaru* | a cloth to wrap about |
| *chalichi* | church | | the body, similar to |
| *chiperoni* | rain which came from | | the Indian sari, con- |
| | a certain direction in | | taining about seven |
| | Nyasaland, now | | yards of goods |
| | Malawi | *nsima* | a coarse, half-cooked, |
| *cimanga* | maize or corn | | unsalted porridge |
| *dona* | madam | | made of water and |
| *gogo* | grandmother or grand- | | cornmeal |
| | father | *ntedza* | groundnuts (peanuts) |
| *gome* | boys' compound | *nthoci* | banana or hands of |
| *impala* | a type of antelope | | bananas |
| *inu* | respectful form of say- | *Nyasaland* | former British colony, |
| | ing "you" | | now independent |
| *iwe* | you | | and renamed Malawi |
| *kalulu* | hare | *okondedwa* | beloved |
| *khonde* | porch or veranda | *paraffin* | kerosene |
| *kupemphera* | pray | *potsherd* | a broken piece of a |
| *kupysopysona* | kissing, to nibble and | | water pot |
| | gnaw | *Sabata* | Sabbath |
| *Lake Nyasa* | now Lake Malawi | *singano* | needle |
| *linthumbu* | driver ants | *sjambok* | rhinoceros whip |
| *lobola* | cattle, goats, fowls, or | *skulu* | school |
| | money received as | *tata* | father |
| | the bride-price | *thonje* | thread or cotton |
| *mafuta* | oil | *ticky bazaar* | a store similar to the |
| *maize* | corn | | American ten-cent |
| *matabwa* | lumber | | store |
| *mealie* | maize | *Tsalani bwino* | Remain in peace |
| *mnqusho* | hominy | | (way of saying good- |
| *mowa* | liquor | | bye) |
| *mpango* | scarf or head covering | *tsukambale* | kitchen assistant, or |
| *mphanda* | girls' compound | | literally, plate- |
| *mtwala* | beer | | washer |
| *Musalire* | Do not cry, beautiful | *ubaba* | father |
| *wokongola* | one | *umame* | mother |
| *Msisya* | a tribe living by Lake | *Vypsya* | the country around |
| | Malawi | | northern Nyasaland |
| *namwali* | maiden | | highlands |
| *Nanunso* | You, too | *wacifundo* | merciful one |
| *ndege* | airplane | *wokondedwa* | beloved |
| *ndi mimba* | pregnant | *wokongola* | beautiful one |
| *ndiwo* | a salty food to be eaten | *yanu* | respectful form of |
| | with *nsima* | | "yours" |